"Being a physician and caring for critically ill patients is not always fun, but it challenges our basic life assumptions and stretches us to be fuller persons. Reading *Glimmers of Grace* will teach you some medicine, but even more, it will model how to reflect on the difficulties of life by meditating on Scripture. In beautiful, almost poetic prose, Dr. Butler shares her thoughts on life in the hospital—its struggles, tragedies, and victories. Read this book slowly and pray that God will use it to transform you, helping you see your own challenges in light of Scripture. He will!"

John Dunlop, MD, Internal Medicine, Geriatrics, Yale School of Medicine; author, *Finishing Well to the Glory of God*

"As a father of two sons in the medical field and as a pastor who's tried to help people learn to lament, I'm thankful for *Glimmers of Grace*. It's a rare glimpse into both the spiritual struggles of being a surgeon and how to think biblically through relentless tragedy. Honest, candid, and hopeful, this book demonstrates how to embrace scriptural truth while living in a fallen world. *Glimmers of Grace* is not just for doctors and nurses—it's for anyone learning to trust God through suffering."

Mark Vroegop, Lead Pastor, College Park Church, Indianapolis, Indiana; author, *Dark Clouds, Deep Mercy* and *Weep with Me*

"This book combines the two qualities so often missing from our culture's approach to suffering and death: brutal honesty and resilient hope. That's because Butler writes from unique experience in the valley of the shadow of death. And she writes of the God whose rod and staff are our only comfort."

Matt McCullough, Pastor, Edgefield Church, Nashville, Tennessee; author, *Remember Death: The Surprising Path to Living Hope*

"In the heartrending theater of trauma medicine, Kathryn Butler discovers parables and signs pointing to the God who loves, suffers, and heals. This book is for all who will suffer injury, illness, and death, including their clinicians. May we have ears to hear and eyes to see."

Farr Curlin, MD, Josiah Trent Professor of Medical Humanities; Codirector, Theology, Medicine, and Culture Initiative, Duke University

"Gritty and grace-filled, this book offers much-needed perspective on suffering. As a trauma surgeon, Kathryn Butler has walked with the grieving, wrestling with the tension between the goodness of God and the reality of life in this broken world. Her honest questions as she learned to lean on God's word and trust his character will make *Glimmers of Grace* a blessing to many."

Vaneetha Rendall Risner, author, *Walking through Fire: A Memoir of Loss and Redemption*

"We spend our hardest moments in hospitals, whether with family or friends or in the bed ourselves. How many have here lost the faith they thought they had—or found the Christ they never expected? Kathryn Butler has walked these floors, performed the surgeries, delivered the worst news, and watched patients die—not only as a doctor but also as a Christian. She, of course, is not the only one, but what is rare is her heart and ability to communicate what she's learned to others. Many doctors have had these experiences, fewer have had them as Christians, and fewer still have been willing to write about them and been able to do so with such skill. It's only a matter of time until you find yourself in a hospital again. Will you be ready to lean on God's word for the particular ways he meets us in illness?"

David Mathis, Senior Teacher and Executive Editor, desiringGod.org; Pastor, Cities Church, Saint Paul, Minnesota; author, *Habits of Grace*

Glimmers of Grace

Glimmers of Grace

*A Doctor's Reflections on Faith, Suffering,
and the Goodness of God*

Kathryn Butler, MD

CROSSWAY®

WHEATON, ILLINOIS

Library of Congress Cataloging-in-Publication Data

Names: Butler, Kathryn, 1980– author.
Title: Glimmers of grace : a doctor's reflections on faith, suffering, and the goodness of God / Kathryn Butler.
Description: Wheaton, Illinois : Crossway, [2021] | Includes bibliographical references and index.
Identifiers: LCCN 2020028553 (print) | LCCN 2020028554 (ebook) | ISBN 9781433570483 (trade paperback) | ISBN 9781433570513 (pdf) | ISBN 9781433570506 (mobi) | ISBN 9781433570490 (epub)
Subjects: LCSH: Sick—Religious life. | Sick—Prayers and devotions. | Suffering—Religious aspects—Christianity. | Grief—Religious aspects—Christianity. | God (Christianity)—Goodness. | Butler, Kathryn, 1980– | Christian physicians—United States—Anecdotes.
Classification: LCC BV4910 .B88 2021 (print) | LCC BV4910 (ebook) | DDC 248.8/6—dc23
LC record available at https://lccn.loc.gov/2020028553
LC ebook record available at https://lccn.loc.gov/2020028554

For David, my brother in heaven and a light of grace to so many.
We love you, dear friend. Rejoice before the throne.

Contents

PART 3: BY GRACE YOU HAVE BEEN SAVED:
REMEMBERING WHAT GOD HAS DONE

Introduction

Fear not, for I have redeemed you;
   I have called you by name, you are mine.
When you pass through the waters, I will be with you;
   and through the rivers, they shall not overwhelm you.

ISAIAH 43:1–2

MIDWAY THROUGH MY surgical training, a single night's work in the emergency department shattered my belief in God.

I was a nominal Christian, with an understanding of God grounded more in sentimentality than biblical truth. One night, too many hearts thudded to a stop beneath my hands, and my tenuous belief unraveled. After work the next morning I felt hollowed out, as if a vital part of me had torn out from its roots. Although my body ached for rest, I drove two hours from home in desperation to reconnect with something good and true.

It was one of those gorgeous October days that sets New England aglow in jewel tones. I stopped at a bridge in the Berkshire Mountains, where the Connecticut River wound blue and pearl-flecked between hills afire with color. Amidst this brilliance I shut my eyes to pray.

No words came. Through closed lids I saw only the blood staining my gloves, a boy's eyes fixed in his final gaze. I heard his mother scream as she crumpled to the floor in grief.

I opened my eyes and scanned a horizon glittering with God's fingerprints. I yearned for certainty of his goodness to course through me like lightning, to penetrate to my bones.

But no faith sparked within me. Instead, questions haunted me: *How could people look at one another, and see no value? How could God allow such evil? How could he permit suffering to ravage people who love their families and dream of happiness and hope for something better, as we all do?*

When I returned to the hospital the next morning, I completed my rounds as always. I attended to my patients as usual, scrolled through the black-and-white images of CT scans, and peeled back dressings from wounds. But within, my heart was hardened. My limbs moved in their perfunctory work, but my mind remained on that bridge, pining for the God whom I'd abandoned.

Hope in the Wilderness

My struggle with faith in the hospital is hardly unique. Over years of walking alongside patients, colleagues, and friends during illness, I've witnessed how illness can threaten our grasp of God's love. We may sing God's praises with fervor in church, but when we can't breathe, or when pain seizes us, or when yet another procedure fails to cure, his presence can seem remote.

Even if disease doesn't strike us firsthand, all of us flounder in its shockwaves. Perhaps you've sat at the bedside of a dying loved one, and while memorizing the creases of a beloved hand you can't bear to release, you've agonized about God's plan amid all the hurt. Or maybe you've dedicated your life to caring for the sick, and you regularly question God's compassion when children die or when catastrophic accidents rob families of those they love. *Where is God in all this?* you wonder. *Why doesn't he seem to answer when I pray?* Whether you're walking through illness firsthand, journeying alongside a loved one, or caring for the ill, the hospital can plunge you into your darkest hours, luring you into doubts about God's love, perhaps even about his existence.

No glib answers can alleviate such hurts. Nothing the world offers can erase the anguish when heart tracings flatline, or sponge away our questions when pain incapacitates us. Our only hope, and our satisfaction, derives from cleaving with all our heart and mind and soul to the truths in Scripture: that God is "merciful and gracious, slow to anger, and abounding in steadfast love and faithfulness" (Ex. 34:6), and that he "so loved the world, that he gave his only Son, that whoever believes in him should not perish but have eternal life" (John 3:16).

Even when despair obscures our vision of God, Scripture assures us *he is there.* He is holy and merciful, the great "I AM" who provides manna from heaven to feed the hungry (Ex. 3:14; 16:4; 34:6). In love the Father gave his only begotten Son for us (John 3:16). In love, that same Son now advocates for us when the wages of sin threaten to subdue us (1 John 2:1–2; Rom. 8:34; Eph. 2:4–7). He walks with us when our bodies languish and break, when our hopes crumble and scatter like brittle leaves in the wind (Ps. 34:18). When the floodwaters rise, he holds us above the waves (Isa. 43:2). He, too, has known deep suffering (Isa. 53:3) and embraces us in love no matter what bad news we bear or what fears we face. In him, we have forgiveness. In him, we have life beyond the confines of our dying, mortal shells (1 Cor. 15:55).

Even when afflictions assail us and we trudge heavy-laden through corridors where antiseptic and protocols prevail, God's goodness remains unchanged. His love for us in Christ endures. His faithfulness never fails.

When sin afflicts us body and soul, we draw our only hope from God's inspired word. Only through his word do we remember who he is and what he has accomplished for us in Christ, out of love for us. And when we remember the promises God has fulfilled and look forward to the promises he assures, the narratives of our lives bloom with examples of grace.

An Invitation to Remember

In *Glimmers of Grace*, I invite you to join me in remembering God's steadfast love, which covers us even during medical calamities. As I prayed about writing this book, verses from Scripture that emphasized remembrance repeatedly surfaced to mind: Joshua building the memorial of twelve stones (Josh. 4:1–7); a dying Moses pleading with his people to remember God's deeds (Deut. 4:9); Asaph turning to his memory of God's work to sustain him through despair (Ps. 77:9–11); Jesus, on the eve of his death, urging us to remember him with the wine and the bread (Luke 22:19). Such passages reveal that when we remember God's mercy, we learn to discern his guiding hand where once we saw only sorrow. We perceive glimmers of grace burning through the dark like unfading stars.

This book drastically differs from my first, *Between Life and Death*. In that work I sought to provide practical guidance, and so I heavily annotated the text with research studies and bullet points. In contrast, *Glimmers of Grace* emphasizes testimony and devotion, as I aim to steward the narratives with which God has entrusted me during my years in medicine. As Jackie Hill Perry so beautifully states, through this book "I invite you into my worship."[1]

Most of the following chapters include stories from my own experiences as a critical care surgeon and as a friend coming alongside the sick, intertwined with exegesis of Scripture. Devotional chapters, titled in italics, interweave with the vignettes and focus on how mundane routines in medicine—intravenous fluids, blood transfusions, and so on—can trigger our memory of God's grace. These shorter chapters close in prayer and reflect my own plea that the Holy Spirit would give us hearts to understand and eyes to see God's love at work, even in the everyday drudgery of the hospital (Deut. 29:4).

Glimmers of Grace unfolds in three parts. In the first, we'll explore in broad brushstrokes how medical settings can challenge our faith. In part 2 we'll mine the Bible for *who God is*, while part 3 considers *what God has done for us*, especially through Jesus's death and resurrection. Finally, the appendixes provide practical content, including a glossary and a list of verses to memorize before illness strikes.

Throughout the book I've changed identifying factors including names, diagnoses, and gender to protect privacy. The stories and the dialogue, however, are as accurate as my notes and memory allow. I've devoted special attention to the testimony of my late friend David, who in six months taught me more about faith in the face of illness than I learned in over a decade of doctoring. I'm deeply grateful to his family, especially his sister Roxi—now a sister to me!—for permitting me to share his story, and for reviewing pertinent chapters.

1   Jackie Hill Perry, *Gay Girl, Good God* (Nashville, B&H Books, 2018), 192.

My hope in the pages that follow is to encourage you that even during the most harrowing moments in the hospital, God's hold on you remains firm. As he parted the waters of the Red Sea before Moses's staff (Ex. 14:21–22), so also through Christ he clears a path for us, guiding us away from the enslavement of our failing bodies toward eternal communion with him.

Please join me in remembering that in Christ, our awesome, loving God has sapped even death of its sting (1 Cor. 15:55). When the heartbeat quickens and the monitor alarm sounds, God remains faithful, gracious, and merciful, abounding in steadfast love and faithfulness (Ex. 34:6). Things may fall apart. The waters will rise. You may grip a bridge railing and yearn for rescue. But in Christ, God's love will always buoy you through the storm, and through his word, glimmers of his grace will pierce the gloom.

PART 1

———————

WANDERING IN THE WILDERNESS

*He knows your going through this great wilderness. These forty years the L*ORD *your God has been with you.*

DEUTERONOMY 2:7

1

I Will Declare Your Greatness

They shall speak of the might of your awesome deeds,
and I will declare your greatness.

"YOU NEED TO come in." I heard her draw a breath. We'd walked together through so many terrible months that I could picture her hand on her forehead, the creases at her eyes deepening as she raked her fingers through her hair. We'd shared upsetting phone calls before, but this time was different. In the gathering quiet between us, I could tell she knew it too.

"How much time do I have?" she asked, her voice cracking. "I'm over half an hour away. Do I have that long?"

I glanced at her husband's monitor. His oxygen levels were dangerously low. The tracing of his heart activity spasmed, threatening to pitch into a fatal rhythm.

"Please just come as soon as you can," I said.

Back at his bedside, the nurses and I fought to keep him alive. We pushed medications to prod his heart to contract and his blood vessels to squeeze. We gave him blood and calcium, and corrected the levels of acid that steadily leached into his bloodstream. His respiratory therapist hovered at the ventilator beside him, adjusting the volume and pressure of each mechanical breath.

But the numbers would not rebound. They continued their steady decline, and soon his skin turned mottled from insufficient oxygen. I performed a bronchoscopy, and saw blood pooling into his bronchial tree. I suctioned it free, and felt a flicker of hope as I glimpsed the pearly surface of his airways, but then blood surged into the field again.

We could not keep up.

The dismal numbers continued to blink on the monitor. I thought about all the months he had struggled, the surgeries, the catastrophes. The moments with loved ones lost. The pain. All the while, his wife had held vigil beside him. Sometimes, stretched to the breaking point, she snapped at nurses and doctors, and guarded her fragile heart with words. At other moments the suffering so bore down on her that she was stoic, her heart compressed into stone, the way pressure hardens delicate shells into limestone and then marble. Throughout, she was steadfast in her devotion to him. She would sit beside him for hours, even while he faded in and out of a medication-induced haze, even when he no longer recognized her.

After all they'd endured together, he was now proceeding across the threshold without her. He was dying, and she was stuck in traffic.

Please, Lord, let him hold on until she arrives, I prayed over and over. *Please don't take him until she's said goodbye. They've been through so much. Please let them be together one last time.*

I stared at the monitor, but struggled to focus. Its lines blurred. I waited for the alarms to sound, for his heart to finally limp to a stop. His nurse, too, waited. Our hands, always so frenetic, now itched from sudden inactivity, but there was nothing we could do. We waited for the alarms. I paced back and forth, praying. I pleaded for God to grind the hands of time to a stop, to reverse the laws of physics for just this moment. I prayed that somehow the rows of cars that cluttered Boston could part like the Red Sea before Moses's staff, the taillights aligned into two glowing processions, and allow his wife through. That she could say goodbye.

Still, his heart beat. Still, he held on.

His nurse and I both looked at each other in disbelief. The numbers hung abysmally low. His meager oxygen levels couldn't sustain him. Yet still, he lived.

For another half an hour.

Finally his wife burst into the room, her jacket still zipped to her chin. She pushed past us, and grasped his hand. Her fingers interlocked with those she'd loved as a newlywed, and which she'd massaged when illness contorted and discolored them beyond recognition.

At that exact moment, his heart stopped. The alarm sounded.

I drifted from the room, sadness weighing down my steps, and incredulity gripping my chest. The memories from the last hours tumbled through my mind, cresting and breaking like waves against the shore.

He'd held on until *the moment* she'd touched him. Against all odds. Against everything the statistics and the rules and the workings of physiology would dictate, he'd held on. His oxygen levels were so low that his blood had turned to acid. His proteins had uncoiled, his enzymes halted their work. The envelopes encasing his cells had split open and spilled his DNA from their pores. Death draped over him like a pallid cloak.

But God (Eph. 2:4). God ushered him through that dark valley. God walked with him, even while the blood frothed in his lungs, even while life ebbed away. Out of mercy. Out of love, and out of mercy.

Christ bore the same torrent of blood and water and cried out for his Father, but he died alone. And that same God, who gave his Son for us, gazed upon a man alone in a bed, life dwindling from his ghastly body, and granted him mercy. One last handhold. One last touch.

This was an answer to prayer.

I was shaking. The only appropriate response was to worship, to fall to my knees and thank God for his steadfast love, for being who he is—the great "I AM," the one who saves. It was a moment to proclaim to all those who could hear. It was a moment worthy of ten thousand hallelujahs: *Look, what our Lord has done! He who is mighty has done great things for me, and holy is his name* (Luke 1:49).

But I didn't praise him. I didn't kneel, sing, or pray. I didn't rejoice at how God had made himself known, how his grace had filled a hospital room as his robes once billowed through the temple (Isa. 6:1). I said nothing about God's work that day in the ICU.

Instead, my pager went off, and I went back to work. There were nineteen more sick patients to see. There wasn't time to pause, or to reflect.

And in the hospital, we don't talk about such things.

The Wilderness of Medicine

Modern medicine enables healing at rates unprecedented in history. HIV is now a chronic condition, rather than a death sentence. Improved treatments and resuscitation techniques have dramatically reduced mortality rates from severe infections. We surgeons can now perform gallbladder and colon operations through tiny incisions, freeing patients to return home in a day or two rather than weeks after surgery.

Yet for all its merits, the field of medicine often ignores the human dimensions of disease, especially the questions illness stirs up about faith. In medical school, my peers and I learned to trace out the courses of vessels and nerves, and to glean meaning from the concentrations of salts and molecules in the bloodstream, but we learned nothing about how illness compels us to grieve, to pray, and to search for meaning. We cultivated fluency in medical jargon but were left with no vocabulary for suffering, faith, or empathy. And so when your heart cries out for help in the hospital, my colleagues and I are more likely to check your labs than to partner with you in your pain.

In my first year of medical school, hints of this disconnect between the science and the humanity of medicine prompted me to chuck my anatomy textbook against a wall. I'd been drowning in test preparation for weeks, and unfamiliar terminology slowed my progress as I repeatedly stopped to cross-reference a medical dictionary. Finally, the word *decussate* pushed my aggravation to the brink. A quick heave, and the book slammed against the wall of my dorm room and slid, mangled, to the floor.

"Why can't they just say *cross over*?" I shouted to the air. "How can I talk with patients when medicine is a foreign language?" I'd majored in biochemistry in college, and so was accustomed to scholarly discussions within laboratories, but I knew medicine reaches beyond the realm of microscopes and pipettes, into the lives of people who are scared and hurting. Wouldn't technical language distance me from the very people I sought to help?

I vowed thereafter to always maintain my compassion, and to never lose sight of each individual as unique, layered, and loved by God.

Yet years later, when a census of forty patients to see by seven in the morning became the norm, I too morphed into the aloof, detached doctor—all science, scant humanity—I'd so loathed becoming. This humbling reality struck me at the end of my chief year of surgery residency, when my interns roasted me with a video during a graduation assembly. In the clip, an actress portrayed me barreling down the hallway on my morning rounds and shoving others out of my way like a bulldozer. Advisors and mentees in the audience snickered. I squirmed in my seat. Like most parodies, the depiction was funny and humiliating, because it echoed the truth.

Despite my pledge to the contrary, I'd learned to prioritize efficiency over tenderness, and hard, cold data over the content of people's hearts. As laughter in the crowd died down, I wondered how many people with hard questions I'd stranded for the sake of expediency. I wondered how many concerns I'd dismissed, how many souls I'd left wounded when, too busy to pause, I'd poked incisions, listened to lungs, and with a cool sense of duty marched on to the next patient.

If research offers any insight, the answer is probably a lot. Surveys show that although patients often seek spiritual support from their doctors,[1] we routinely ignore their requests.[2] In a culture rooted in science and secularism, medical staff find faith discussions uncom-

---

1 Michael J. Balboni et al., "Nurse and Physician Barriers to Spiritual Care Provision at the End of Life," *Journal of Pain and Symptom Management* 48, no. 3 (2014): 400–410.

2 Natalie C. Ernecoff et al., "Health Care Professionals' Responses to Religious or Spiritual Statements by Surrogate Decision Makers During Goals-of-Care Discussions," *JAMA Internal Medicine* 175, no. 10 (2015): 1662–69.

fortable, even unwelcome. If we do listen, too often we conflate the humanistic with the spiritual, offering a handhold when our patients ask for prayer.[3] Spiritual questions *are* outside the scope of doctors and nurses when undertaken alone, especially when beliefs conflict. The expertise of a hospital chaplain is essential. But here's the problem: *we doctors don't even refer patients to chaplaincy.* In one multicenter study of terminally ill cancer patients, 85 percent expressed spiritual concerns, but only *1 percent* reported that their doctors had referred them to chaplaincy.[4] Nurses fared better, but still not stellar, with a referral rate of only 4 percent.[5] Studies show that when we do think of chaplaincy, physicians usually seek out help for patients in the last day or two of life, to people actively dying, on breathing machines, and unable to communicate.[6] While we so diligently attend to the cadence of the heartbeat and the concentration of potassium, doctors abandon people with crippling questions about the meaning behind their ordeal. Medical school teaches future doctors much about the body, but precious little about how to guide people when illness fractures the soul.

The disconnect is troubling, because illness doesn't begin or end with biological processes run amok. A hospital stay wrenches us from our homes, vocations, and families. It places life on hold, afflicts us with loneliness and despair, and challenges our convictions about life, death, suffering, and the goodness of God.

---

3   Michael J. Balboni and Tracy A. Balboni, *Hostility to Hospitality: Spirituality and Professional Socialization within Medicine* (New York, Oxford University Press, 2019), 29, 65.

4   Balboni and Balboni, *Hostility to Hospitality*, 58–59, 65.

5   Balboni and Balboni, *Hostility to Hospitality*, 65.

6   Philip J. Choi, Farr A. Curlin, and Christopher E. Cox, "The Patient is Dying, Please Call the Chaplain: The Activities of Chaplains in One Medical Center's Intensive Care Units," *Journal of Pain and Symptom Management* 50 no. 4 (2015): 501–6.

As chaplains James Gibbons and Sherry Miller so aptly stated decades ago:

> Hospitals are far more than biological garages where dysfunctional human parts are repaired or replaced. They are rather places where patients, and their loved ones, come face-to-face with their vulnerability, their finitude, and ultimately their mortality. As such, hospitals are places of anguishing ambiguity. [Patients] journey along a path with hope and healing ranged along one side, while terror and tragedy threaten on the other.[7]

Although we try to buffer ourselves with science, those of us in stethoscopes and white coats walk this path, too. We witness the suffering of the ill and lie awake at night. Guilt floods us as we remember the child, the mother, or the grandfather we couldn't save. We analyze our mistakes and replay harrowing scenes in our minds, and their sickening impact tears our hearts open. We too wonder, *Where is God in all this? Where is he, amid the calamity and the loss?*

Yet while caught up in the bustle of medical care, we remain silent. Even when our faith breaks and crumbles, we don't voice our questions. Even when we witness God's mercy in an ICU room, when he prods the heart of a dying man to beat a while longer, we keep our prayers and our praises to ourselves.

I Will Declare Your Greatness

For far too long, as a professional steeped in a secular system, I've witnessed God's greatness in silence. I've let the questions of the

---

7   James L. Gibbons and Sherry L. Miller, "An Image of Contemporary Hospital Chaplaincy," *Journal of Pastoral Care* 43, no. 4 (1989): 355–61.

suffering hang in the air, and the gospel memories of dying believers grow dim.

Christ calls us to more.

In the Gospel of John, Jesus warned his apostles that the world would despise them, and promised the following: "But when the Helper comes, whom I will send to you from the Father, the Spirit of truth, who proceeds from the Father, he will bear witness about me. And you also will bear witness, because you have been with me from the beginning" (John 15:26–27). Note the exhortation to *bear witness*. Those of us who know Christ and whom God has anointed with the Spirit are called to proclaim who he is and what he has done. The Christian walk mustn't proceed in silence.

The book of Acts reveals that the apostles heeded Jesus's command under the most dangerous of circumstances. In chapter 4, the priests and Sadducees arrested John and Peter for preaching about Christ's resurrection. If you or I were in the same situation, we'd likely keep quiet to avoid further trouble. Yet the truth burned so brightly in their hearts that Peter and John declared, "We cannot but speak of what we have seen and heard" (Acts 4:20)!

Their proclamation guides us to declare the Lord's deeds to our brothers and sisters even in environments hostile to his word. When our fervor for God overflows, not only do we glorify God's name, but also we take hold of the biblical truth that *God is there*, working all for good (Rom 8:28). His hand covers us in the midst of the pain, the sedatives, and the decaying of our bodies. While a ventilator sighs for us, or cancer invades spaces it doesn't own, God remains with us (Matt. 28:20). "Where shall I go from your Spirit?" sings David. "Or where shall I flee from your presence? / If I ascend to heaven, you are there! / If I make my bed in Sheol, you are there! / If I take the wings of the morning / and dwell in the uttermost parts of the sea, / even there your hand shall lead me, / and your right hand shall hold me" (Ps. 139:7–10).

God's hand, the same that heaped up the crystal-capped peaks of the Himalayas and molded us from dust, leads us through the tempests that afflict us. This side of the cross he promises that the aches and the heaviness, the bruises and the wounds that trouble these bodies now will eventually fade away, washed clean in the blood of Christ (Rev. 21:4–6).

Psalm 145 teaches us that when we bear witness to God's greatness, we make him known and illuminate his promises. We remind one another of who God is: "The LORD is gracious and merciful, / slow to anger and abounding in steadfast love. / The LORD is good to all, / and his mercy is over all that he has made" (Ps. 145:8–9). We also remind one another of how the Lord walks with us in the wilderness:

> The LORD upholds all who are falling
> and raises up all who are bowed down.
> The eyes of all look to you,
> and you give them their food in due season.
> You open your hand;
> you satisfy the desire of every living thing.
> The LORD is righteous in all his ways
> and kind in all his works.
> The LORD is near to all who call on him,
> to all who call on him in truth.
> He fulfills the desire of those who fear him;
> he also hears their cry and saves them.
> The LORD preserves all who love him,
> but all the wicked he will destroy.

My mouth will speak the praise of the LORD,
and let all flesh bless his holy name forever and ever.
(Ps. 145:14–21)

We brothers and sisters in Christ need these reminders. We need to know, when the heavy days plod on without relief, that the Lord is near. When we undergo yet another test or wince through yet another needle stick, we need to remember that he upholds the falling and raises up the bowed down.

Too often, the technical routines of the hospital and the checklists of busy clinicians hide such reminders from view. You may thirst for God, for the cool comfort of his word, but settle for a mouth swab. You may wrangle with questions that steal your breath, but your doctor, too overwhelmed to pause, listens to your chest, shrugs, and hurries on.

In the pages that follow, I humbly aim to pause, to attend, and at long last to speak of what I've seen and heard. When we delve into Scripture, we see that God hears and heeds the cries of his people wandering in the wilderness, be it in the wind-whipped desolation of ancient Arabia or in the monitoring unit of a cardiology wing. His grace in Christ penetrates the lonely corners of the hospital even when no one acknowledges his guiding hand. Even when catheters and monitoring wires entangle you, and even when those around you speak in a foreign language, "the LORD upholds all who are falling / and raises up all who are bowed down" (Ps. 145:14).

When fear and anguish shake you, he holds you in his righteous hand.

When medical techniques falter, his love for you in Christ never will.

Please join me in declaring his greatness, so we may remember.

2

I Will Remember Your Wonders

"Has God forgotten to be gracious?
Has he in anger shut up his compassion?"
Then I said, "I will appeal to this,
to the years of the right hand of the Most High.
I will remember the deeds of the LORD;
yes, I will remember your wonders of old."

PSALM 77:9–11

"I JUST WANT to go to heaven," he said.

I studied David's eyes. We'd weathered heavy moments before, in similar hospital rooms with curtain dividers and tray tables littered with Jell-O cups. I would ply my kids with activity books while he and I leaned over sandwiches or fried chicken (he insisted on dark meat), and we would talk about the undulating course of his illness, the constant cycling between hospital, rehab, and back again. We'd drift into banter about church happenings, crack a few Daffy Duck jokes, and then dialogue about God, faith, and hope. Hard topics weren't new. They seemed to weave through our discussions like water between river stones.

Yet as he stared into some lonely place I couldn't see or understand, his dejection unsettled me.

"David, you mean you're *ready* to go to heaven?"

"No, I'm not ready. What I mean is that I don't know if that's where I'm going. I just keep asking God over and over to forgive me. I'm so scared."

I felt the blood drain from my face. Ever since God's grace touched him in a grimed alleyway of New York City decades earlier, David had devoted his life to witnessing for Christ. He spoke the truth in love to roommates struggling with addiction. He recounted his past trials with substance abuse to guide troubled teenagers into God's embrace. He tended a memorial garden abloom with sunflowers so that friends dying of HIV would know that they, too, were image bearers of God, that they were loved, and that others would remember them.

Even when his emphysema flared, David would minister to his church through emails praising God. He saw his hospitalizations as opportunities for witness, and during each admission he would pray for his roommates and distribute Spanish-translation Bibles to cleaning staff. "Please bring me more Bibles to hand out," he'd ask during phone calls. "There are people here who still don't know Jesus!" During all his ordeals, David had never lost sight of God's love for him.

Until that day. After all he'd been through, after all he'd withstood, he doubted his salvation while my kids scribbled in coloring books on his hospital bed.

I gripped his hand. "Do you believe Jesus died for you?"

He breathed to the limit of his scar-encased lungs. A moment passed. Two.

"Yes," he finally answered.

"Then David, *you are forgiven*. In the midst of all of this—the good news and the bad, the uncertainty of what's coming—the one thing that's absolutely sure, is that you'll be with Jesus. That's the single thing you can be certain of. And it's what matters most."

Our eyes locked. Relief washed over me when he gave a slight nod, but in the next instant his eyelids drooped closed. "I know this is going to happen again," he said. By "this," he meant another call to 911, another long hospitalization. Another spell during which his body broke down, and with it, the life he loved.

I hugged him, and felt the rattle of his breath through his inflamed airways. We prayed together, and lingered for a moment. The cures had run out, and in the desolation of illness, only prayer was left. Only God could heal what medical gadgetry couldn't touch. Only Christ, bleeding upon the cross, knew such suffering, and lent meaning to it.

A Light to My Path

David had shuttled back and forth between rehab and the hospital for months, often confused, sometimes strapped to breathing machines, seldom returning to the spaces that infused his life with meaning. Amid the fear, monotony, and disappointments, all the memories of God's work in his life started to blur. He would try to read the Bible, but sleep deprivation and chronic low oxygen muddled his concentration. "I can't understand what I'm reading," he'd say. "The words just swim on the page."

Soon, the looming threat of death edged Christ out of his thoughts. The brother whose love for Christ always overflowed, who ministered to others even when he could barely breathe, sat bereft, his hand in mine, despairing about his own salvation.

Trials in the hospital do this. In whatever capacity you encounter medicine, the hospital acquaints you with suffering and pain, grief and fear. Illness confronts us with troubling questions about life, mortality, the future, and even eternity, and we feel ill-equipped to answer them in the crucible of the hospital.

Before illness claims our days, spiritual routines provide us with an anchor, a sturdy, deep-rooted tree for us to grasp. The church calendar, traditions, and liturgy echo Scripture, and offer "a lamp to my feet and a light to my path" (Ps. 119:105). When we lift our voices in praise, the verses we sing overcome doubts. We read of Jonah pursued and saved in a storm, and marvel at God's mercy. We kneel beside Jesus in the garden of Gethsemane, share in his tears, and swell with gratitude that he, too, knows deep suffering. We collapse before him at the terrible silhouette of the cross, and our souls cry out, awed by his love for us.

But from what do we draw strength when we spend our Sundays confined to a hospital bed? How do we draw solace from the Bible when medications impair our ability to read? When procedures, needles, and disability cut us off from the spiritual rhythms we hold dear, assurances of God's love similarly evade us.

As an example, consider my friend who recently survived a medical crisis. A fiercely independent woman who built houses for fun, she returned home from the hospital unable to drive, cook, read, or balance a checkbook. With her self-sufficiency gone, she sank into discouragement, and yearned for the reassurance of God's promises in Scripture. But when she turned to her Bible, she could no longer decode the words. When I'd offer to clean her house or buy groceries, she always answered with the same plea: "Can you please just pray with me? It's the only thing that helps."

The body of Christ is essential during such trials. Illness stamps out memories of God's goodness, and severs us from the practices that steep us in his word. As brothers and sisters in Christ, our role is to guide the ill toward the life-giving waters again (John 7:38). Our role is to help them remember.

On Remembering

Even a cursory study of the Bible reveals a link between remembrance and worship. In the Old Testament, the patriarchs and the prophets warned the Israelites to cherish their memories of God's works, lest they forget his steadfast love and pursue idols. They issued these warnings with good reason: during the exodus, God freed his people from slavery, parted the Red Sea, and supplied food from heaven, yet the Israelites forgot the Lord and placed their hope in things forged with their own hands (Ex. 32:3–4). On the horizon of his own death, Moses urged the people whom he'd shepherded for forty years to "take care, and keep your soul diligently, lest you *forget* the things that your eyes have seen" (Deut. 4:9). Their grumbling in the wilderness warns us that when we forget who God is and what he has done, we can no longer discern *him*, and risk straying from the path.

The Psalms also teach us to remember God when we suffer. In Psalm 77, Asaph laments, "Will the LORD spurn forever, / and never again be favorable? / Has his steadfast love forever ceased?" (Ps. 77:7–8). In the midst of his grief, Asaph remembers God's provision, and soon his lamentation turns to praise:

> Then I said, "I will appeal to this,
>   to the years of the right hand of the Most High."
> I will remember the deeds of the LORD;

yes, I will remember your wonders of old.
I will ponder all your work,
    and meditate on your mighty deeds.
Your way, O God, is holy.
    What god is great like our God?
You are the God who works wonders;
    you have made known your might among the peoples.
You with your arm redeemed your people,
    the children of Jacob and Joseph. (Ps. 77:10–15)

Perhaps the most breathtaking call to remember occurs in the upper room, at a modest table spread with bread and bitter herbs. "And he took bread," we read in Luke, "and when he had given thanks, he broke it and gave it to them, saying, 'This is my body, which is given for you. Do this in remembrance of me'" (Luke 22:19). Jesus himself instructs us to partake of bread and wine to stir our memory of him.

Remembrance offers more than wistful nostalgia, and means more than the rapid firings of synapses in our brains. The sacrament of bread and wine teaches us that remembering is worship. When we remember the gospel, we see God's grace at work, unfolding around us, enveloping us in love that burns away the darkness.

Remembering to Love Our Neighbors

When illness cut us off from traditions that kindle our memories, the body of Christ can remind us of God's love. Jesus calls us to love one another not with the pastel sentimentality of greeting cards, but with robust sacrifice (John 13:34). When the vision of a sister fails, we must be her eyes. When a brother's concentration falters, we must guide him through the word. "For as in one body we have many members, and the members do not all have the same function, so we, though many, are one body in Christ, and individually members one of another" (Rom. 12:4–5).

Loving one another requires us to come alongside those who know Christ, and to *remind them of his love* when the shadows descend. Perhaps you record a playlist of beloved hymns for an ailing friend. Maybe you pray aloud with him, and infuse your heavenward pleas with Scripture, or bring your Bible during visits to read when his own eyes fail. Whatever your approach, embrace the call to remember as a communal one. Moses's plea rang out to every Israelite within hearing. Jesus taught over a meal, in the company of those closest to him. This practice of remembering is one all of us need, corporately, so that when calamity strikes, we may hold tight to who he is: our loving Father, the author of life, compassionate and merciful (Ex. 34:6; Ps. 22:3; Acts 3:15). We need to remember, to nourish our souls with the truth of what he has done: "But God, being rich in mercy, because of the great love with which he loved us, even when we were dead in our trespasses, made us alive together with Christ—by grace you have been saved" (Eph. 2:4–5).

My friend David knew who God was. Even while his hands quavered and his mind turned circles, he knew deep in his heart that Christ had secured him a home in heaven. But he needed to remember. Suffering had driven God's mercies from his memory.

By grace, the Lord would remind him.

3

Wonderfully Made

For you formed my inward parts;
  you knitted me together in my mother's womb.
I praise you, for I am fearfully and wonderfully made.
  Wonderful are your works;
  my soul knows it very well.

PSALM 139:13–14

WHEN ALEXANDER GRAHAM BELL recited the "to be or not to be" soliloquy from Hamlet into his telephone at the 1876 World's Fair, he could hardly have predicted that his contraption of brass and wire would evolve into the device we now know: a sleek, pocket-sized computer from which you can call your grandmother, send messages across the globe, check the weather, find directions, read *War and Peace*, and watch flashy Korean music videos. In revolutionizing how we communicate, seek information, and consume, technology has literally changed the face of society.

So too has it transformed the practice of medicine. For millennia, doctors presumed that an imbalance of blood, phlegm, and bile made us sick (a theory that inspired bloodletting until the late eighteenth century). In contrast to such murky speculation, we can now visualize individual white blood cells rolling toward target bacteria and peer into body cavities with electromagnetic waves. We support the kidneys, lungs, and even the heart with machines, remove diseased segments of intestine through incisions only a couple of inches wide, and harness the workings of our own immune system to fight cancer. Thanks to these advances, life expectancy for infants born in the United States has risen from forty-nine years in 1900 to seventy-eight years in 2017, and most people die from the advanced effects of chronic conditions, rather than from the acute infections that claimed the lives of so many in early history.[1] Our ability to engineer life-saving therapies reflects our identity as image bearers (Gen. 1:26), born to create as our Father creates. It also represents God's kindness toward us, an ordinary means of grace he bestows upon us so we may flourish upon the earth (Gen. 1:28).

The Miracle of Design

Yet even our most sophisticated lab-grown remedies can't compete with God's artistry. Our ability to combat disease and prolong life improves each year, and yet we still can't duplicate the precision and elegance with which he weaves us together. Even our very best medical advancements are pale shadows of God's craftsmanship.

Let me give you an example. Imagine you're with a familiar child—a son or daughter, grandchild, niece or nephew. He tumbles to the ground, scrapes his knee, and runs toward you with arms outstretched. You offer a hug and sweep flecks of gravel from the

---

1   Elizabeth Arias and Jiaquan Xu, "United States Life Tables, 2017," *Centers for Disease Control National Vital Statistics Reports* 68 no. 7 (2019): 58.

wound, then clean it with soap and water. You offer a Band-Aid, not so much for the scrape as to soothe the boy's rattled nerves. The embrace and the bandage work their magic, and after a few minutes he forgets the incident and ambles back to the playground. All you offered was reassurance and a Band-Aid. You didn't fuse the skin back together or command the trickle of blood to halt its downward crawl. Yet as you stooped to examine the scrape, platelets signaled to one another to aggregate at the frayed skin edges. They summoned other inflammatory cells to clear the wound of debris and bacteria. As the boy clambered onto the swings and dangled his feet in the wind, these unseen soldiers had already begun to seal the wound with a mesh of fibrin.

In a day the wound will seal over, and in a week it will pull taut with scar and heal completely. Yet you didn't swipe left or right, reconfigure wiring, or compute an algorithm to prompt the cells to lay down that scaffolding. All you did was hug the kid. The rest, in all its intricacy, occurred without your input, through no effort of your own, solely according to God's design.

Even with serious injuries, the majesty of healing remains God's, not ours. Rather than a scrape, let's say your young friend suffers a gash. After applying pressure, you take him to the emergency room, where an eager surgery resident irrigates the wound and stitches it closed. If the doctor is brash, he'll boast about his aesthetic prowess. But truthfully, rather than "cure" the wound, his sutures only align the skin edges to expedite healing, a complicated process that unfolds without his guidance whatsoever. His handiwork prevents infection and minimizes scar, but it's God's handiwork that forges new tissue.

Perhaps no process displays God's genius more elegantly than pregnancy. An expectant mother takes prenatal vitamins, and avoids alcohol, soft cheeses, and her cat's litter box to protect her baby from harm. She's vigilant in everything. Still, for all her heedfulness, she doesn't command her baby's layers of cells to gently fold into human form. All her life she has owned the space that houses her unborn child, but even she cannot reach there to impress the dimple into his left cheek, to shape his ears, or to send blood surging through his tender veins. Only God, who has already programmed each tint and curve of her baby into intertwining DNA strands, can bid the cells to swirl and array, and spark the heart into its lifelong rhythm. She can nurture and carry, but God coaxes life to bloom. "So neither he who plants nor he who waters is anything, but only God who gives the growth" (1 Cor. 3:7).

Echoes of His Work

While they impress when considered in isolation, our medical technologies seem lackluster compared to the intricacy of healing or the wonder of life unfurling in the womb. Medical advancements are life-saving gifts, but they seem clunky and awkward when compared to the architecture our heavenly Father has fashioned.

Consider blood transfusions. Blood products save lives, yet they can't compete with what God has already supplied in our vessels. Our blood is rich with electrolytes, red blood cells, immune cells, clotting factors, enzymes, and molecular signals, all precisely balanced and reliant upon a specific temperature and acidity to function. The "blood" we receive in a transfusion, by contrast, is a processed, refrigerated concentrate of just *one* of these components. Technicians spin donated blood in a centrifuge to separate red blood cells from clotting factors and platelets, and then package and store the red cell fraction in a refrigerator for up to forty-two days. This processing, while it optimizes rapid access, actually deforms the cells, impeding their navigation through capillaries.[2] Stored blood also accumulates high levels of potassium and acid that prove dangerous in massive transfusions, and an anticlotting agent mixed with donated blood deprives the heart of the calcium it needs to pump.[3] Even in small quantities, blood transfusions suppress the immune system and increase the risk of infection.[4]

Such side effects are warranted—indeed, life-saving!—when hemorrhage is severe. However, in the mildest cases of anemia a blood transfusion can sometimes harm more than help. One of my wisest mentors equated a blood transfusion with a two-week-old sandwich: if you're starving, you absolutely need it. But if you're just a bit peckish, is the stale bread and moldy cheese worth it?

Compared with God's craftsmanship, many innovations in medicine resemble two-week-old sandwiches. Ventilators with digital screens and finely-tuned sensors sustain us through surgeries and pneumonia, but they can't replace the gentle mechanics of natural breathing, and in severe illness can actually injure the lungs. We can't reverse the process by which cells become cancerous, so we flood the body with chemotherapy to poison them . . . along with other healthy tissue. The suffix "ectomy," from the Greek *ek* (out) and *temnein* (to cut), concludes the names of most surgical procedures because often our only way to address a diseased organ is to cut it out. Even our simple

2   David A. Hampton et al., "Cryopreserved Red Blood Cells Are Superior to Standard Liquid Red Blood Cells," *Journal of Trauma and Acute Care Surgery* 77 (2014): 20.

3   Kristen C. Sihler and Lena M. Napolitano, "Complications of Massive Transfusion," *CHEST* 137 no. 1 (2010): 209–20.

4   Sihler and Napolitano, "Complications," 214–15.

mixtures of water and salts that we give through an IV are imperfect, and in large volumes can suppress the immune system and worsen bleeding.[5]

Fearfully and Wonderfully Made

By no means should these points dissuade you from medical treatment. Modern medicine is an ordinary means of grace through which God demonstrates his mercy (Isa. 38:21; 1 Tim. 5:23), and even with its limitations, it returns droves of people home to their families after illness. Medicine is a gift from God for us to *steward*, not to discard.

I make these points only so you may draw hope from God's power. As you gaze upon that translucent bag of saline dangling over your head in the hospital, remember that you belong to one who perfects what medicine can only approximate. Whether treatments succeed or fail, you remain throughout in the grip of the Creator, the one who planned the stars and the sea:

> It is he who made the earth by his power,
>> who established the world by his wisdom,
>> and by his understanding stretched out the heavens.
> When he utters his voice, there is a tumult of waters in the
>> heavens,
>> and he makes the mist rise from the ends of the earth.
> He makes lightning for the rain,
>> and he brings forth the wind from his storehouses.
>> (Jer. 10:12–13)

---

5 Galinos Barmparas et al., "Decreasing Maintenance Fluids in Normotensive Trauma Patients May Reduce Intensive Care Unit Stay and Ventilator Days," *Journal of Critical Care* 31 (2016): 201.

This same God, to whom we owe all the splendid depths and summits of the earth, lovingly arranged your every feature before the world knew your name. David captures this breathtaking truth in Psalm 139:

> For you formed my inward parts;
>> you knitted me together in my mother's womb.
> I praise you, for I am fearfully and wonderfully made.
> Wonderful are your works;
>> my soul knows it very well.
> My frame was not hidden from you,
> when I was being made in secret,
>> intricately woven in the depths of the earth.
> Your eyes saw my unformed substance;
> in your book were written, every one of them,
>> the days that were formed for me,
>> when as yet there was none of them. (Ps. 139:13–16)

Before your parents had any inkling of your existence, God had already aligned your DNA into a twenty-thousand-gene recipe for your eye color, your face shape, and your capacities to feel, yearn, and discover. During your third month in the womb, he etched the pads of your fingers with whorls and lines uniquely your own. He molded your lungs, and linked them to your nervous system so that every day you breathe over ten thousand times without even thinking about it. Your heart, a fistful of muscle threaded with nerves, churns five liters of blood throughout your body every minute, beats forty-two million times in a single year, and until the travails of living in a sinful world overwhelm it, never entreats you to cheer it on.

Most remarkable of all, as we read in Psalm 139, this God, so magnificent in his power, seeks intimacy with *us*. "O LORD, you have searched me and known me!" David praises in verse 1. And then in verses 9–10: "If I take the wings of the morning / and dwell in the uttermost parts of the sea, / even there your hand shall lead me, / and your right hand shall hold me."

Such verses highlight that God's exquisite work in creation, especially his creation of humankind, is a shimmering overflow of his love. Before the dawn of the world, the Father loved his Son (John 17:24), and his creation is an outpouring of that radiance. He creates not for pride or for rule or for power, but as a Father who loves his Son and seeks to share his glory. Your heartbeat and breath, your mind and limbs, and all the elegant workings of your body are not merely machines with fleshy parts. Rather, they are labors of the Father's love.

When the sterility and strangeness of the hospital engulfs you, take heart that one far greater enfolds you in his embrace. He has known you since before you drew your first breath, and he crafted the lungs through which you inspired that new draught of air. Whether treatments vanquish disease or fail in their purpose, his steadfast love endures forever (Ps. 118:1). And in Christ, nothing can wrest you from that love (Rom. 8:38–39).

Heavenly Father, our most sophisticated technologies pale in comparison to your artistry as our Creator. Help us to see that whatever hardships we face, our ultimate hope resides in you. Help us to know your love for us, apparent from the design of our bodies and most magnificently proclaimed in our salvation through Christ.

PART 2

———

I AM YOUR GOD: FINDING SOLACE IN WHO GOD IS

Fear not, for I am with you;
  be not dismayed, for I am your God;
I will strengthen you, I will help you,
  I will uphold you with my righteous right hand.

ISAIAH 41:10

4

The Lord Will Provide

Abraham said, "God will provide for himself
the lamb for a burnt offering, my son."

GENESIS 22:8

MY FIRST THOUGHT when paramedics wheeled him into the trauma bay was that he was just a kid. My second was that he looked like he was dying.

His skin was clammy and his pulse faint. I called his name, but he only moaned. Removal of his shirt revealed a single wound beneath his left nipple, a stream of blood threading down his torso. My resident performed a quick ultrasound, and the dancing images confirmed that a clot compressed the chambers of his heart. Their thin walls collapsed with each beat like two palms clapping. If we didn't act quickly, cardiac arrest would follow.

I called the operating room to alert them that we were coming. A nurse secured one last IV. We unlocked the stretcher to wheel him out of the trauma bay.

Then he lost his pulse.

Some snapshots in life are Romans 1 moments. In verses 19–20, Paul writes, "For what can be known about God is plain to them, because God has shown it to them. For his invisible attributes, namely, his eternal power and divine nature, have been clearly perceived, ever since the creation of the world, in the things that have been made."

Any scenario that includes the cry "I don't feel a pulse" is a Romans 1 moment. The words pitch dread into the stomach like a leaden weight. You clamber frantically at the neck, then at the thigh, in search of the familiar thud of a pulse. When you feel none, your mind goes into overdrive. Regardless of the truth claims you espouse, instinct returns you to your origins, and you pray: *Oh please, no God. No, no, no. Please. Not this.*

The emergency medicine team leapt forward and started CPR, while my resident and I splashed antiseptic and opened the boy's chest. Unlike scheduled, routine surgeries in the operating room, this procedure was a frenzied, last-ditch effort to save a life. After a few swipes of the scalpel and the crank of a retractor, we were peering into a space never intended for worldly exposure. The sac surrounding his heart was tense as a balloon, taut with blood. We incised it and scooped out the clot, then delivered his heart into the open air. With the pressure of the clot on his heart relieved, his pulse returned, and oxygen-rich blood again surged throughout his body. A jet of blood spurted from a wound in his right ventricle, where the assailant's knife had penetrated.

With one hand cupping his heart and the other following the curve of a suture needle through the pulsing muscle, I closed the wound, and we finally rushed him to the operating room. There, under conditions more controlled but still urgent, we repaired a rent in his lung and stopped bleeding from his chest wall.

After the surgery, we delivered him into the hands of the ICU team, and I called an aunt who agreed to talk with us. His mother, I learned, wanted nothing to do with him.

"What'd he do now?" his aunt blurted when I called. "You say you're calling from the hospital? Did he get in another fight?"

"Ma'am, he was stabbed in the heart."

She caught her breath. "Is he okay? I mean, is he—"

"Yes, he's alive, and I think he'll be okay. We have to watch him very carefully over the next twenty-four hours, in case he starts to bleed again. But we were able to repair the hole in his heart."

"Oh, thank you!" She started to cry. "He's not a bad kid, he's just made such a mess of his life. Stealing, doing drugs, doing everything he should've known not to do. A few months ago my sister finally had enough, and kicked him out."

"As he recovers, would she be willing to talk to us, and maybe to a social worker about how to help him?"

She paused for a moment. "Let me talk to her first," she said warily. "The boy needs help, that's for certain. But she's been hurt too many times. If it's not done right, she won't listen."

"Thank you so much. I'll be here all night, and I'll call you if anything changes."

"Doctor, you really—you really think he'll be all right?"

My mind returned to the trauma bay, to the pale grip of death upon him. Had the paramedics delayed even a minute or two, he would have died in the ambulance. Had the assault occurred in proximity to a hospital without trauma services, he would have died in the ER. That he survived the emergency procedure was also remarkable, as it saves life in only 30 percent of such cases.[1] He left the operating room with his heart pounding steadily and

---

1   Mark J. Seamon et al., "An Evidence-Based Approach to Patient Selection for Emergency Department Thoracotomy: A Practice Management Guideline from the Eastern Association for the Surgery of Trauma," *Journal of Trauma and Acute Care Surgery*, 79 no. 1 (2015): 159–73; Clay Cothren Burlew et al., "Western Trauma Association Critical Decisions in

his blood pressure stable, while others would have succumbed to cold and diffuse bleeding.

These were too many gifts to be coincidences.

"Yes," I said. "I think he's going to be fine."

Weeks later, the young man returned to the clinic for follow-up. He sat in clean clothes, his hands folded in his lap, his demeanor shy. His incisions had healed, and he could again walk without pain or shortness of breath. Best of all, he had reconciled with his mother, and was living at home.

"I just want to thank you," he said. "Not just for saving my life. This whole thing has changed me. I want to help people the way you guys do. I've gone back to school, and I want to be a nurse."

All the moments of grace—in the trauma bay, in the operating room, and finally in that clinic—converged like notes in a symphony. In the midst of all the violence and the fear, God was present. In the wake of a life gone astray, he was composing a masterpiece to draw a lost son out of the dark.

All seemed lost, but the Lord provided.

The Lord Provided

The almighty God who provided for the young man that day in the trauma bay has provided for his people since the dawn of time.

In Genesis 22:2, God said to Abraham, "Take your son, your only son Isaac, whom you love, and go to the land of Moriah, and offer him there as a burnt offering on one of the mountains of which I shall tell you." Can you imagine Abraham's agony as he climbed Mount Moriah? Isaac was his beloved son, the gift whom God had

---

Trauma: Resuscitative Thoracotomy," *Journal of Trauma and Acute Care Surgery*, 73 no. 6 (2012): 1359–63.

promised despite Abraham's advanced years. God had vowed to bless all the families of the earth through Isaac (Gen. 12:2–3). As a seal of his faithfulness, the Lord commanded Abram to change his name to Abraham, meaning "father of a multitude" (Gen. 17:4–5). Envision Abraham's confusion and turmoil, then, when God commanded him to give up his greatest treasure in sacrifice. What a terrible burden he must have carried in his heart, as he and his son hauled wood up the slope! What anguish gripped him as Isaac dutifully lay down on the pyre, his trust in his father unyielding.

Yet in Abraham's darkest hour, the Lord provided. On the same place where centuries later temples would rise to bring people together with God, the Lord provided a sacrifice in Isaac's place:

> But the angel of the LORD called to him from heaven and said, "Abraham, Abraham!" And he said, "Here I am." He said, "Do not lay your hand on the boy or do anything to him, for now I know that you fear God, seeing that you have not withheld your son, your only son, from me." And Abraham lifted up his eyes and looked, and behold, behind him was a ram, caught in a thicket by his horns. (Gen. 22:11–13)

God's mercy in this moment foreshadows his ultimate provision for humankind. Millennia later, through the promised line of Isaac, the Father would give up his firstborn Son, whom he has loved since before the birth of the world. In adoration of and obedience to his Father, Christ would willingly lay down his life for us (John 10:18). And all this would provide for us miserable sinners an inheritance, an adoption as God's children, so that we too might draw near to God and call him, "Abba, Father" (Eph. 1:11–12; 1 John 3:1; Rom. 8:15).

Jehovah jirah. The Lord provided.

The Lord Will Provide

Provision for his people is in God's character. *It's who he is.* In the garden, when sin sullied his creation, God banished Adam and Eve, but not before he lovingly clothed them (Gen. 3:21). When all the world writhed in wickedness, he protected Noah and provided a means for life to flourish after the flood (Gen. 8:1–2). He supplied manna from heaven for his people in the wilderness (Ex. 16:11–12). He closed the mouths of lions for Daniel (Dan. 6:22), appointed a fish to rescue Jonah (Jonah 1:17), and commanded ravens to feed Elijah (1 Kings 17:4).

When we consider such examples in the Bible, we find assurance that whatever calamities strike us, *God will provide.* In the trauma bay, as my patient's blood flow slowed to a stop, God provided the means to revive him. After he recovered, God worked through his crisis to guide him toward a home and a future. So too when cancers melt away, pain resolves, and infections clear, we witness God's provision for us. Medical science equips us to combat disease, but *God provides* that technology, guides our hands, and intervenes to usher us back to life. Any good news in the hospital is a glimmer of God's grace. Any cure reflects not the power of our own hands, but rather his provision for us, as he wields medicine as an instrument of mercy.

God's provision is most apparent when we recover, but continues even when the cures fail, because *God has provided for us through Christ.* When we were dead in our sins and trespasses, he redeemed us to himself, not through any merit of our own but through grace (Eph. 2:4–7). Death is the enemy (1 Cor. 15:26), the wages of our sin (Rom. 6:23), but *it is not the end*, because God has triumphed over death and saved us through Christ.

Jesus has pried the menacing grasp of sin from us, and released us from bondage.

Even when tragedy strikes, when sin maims all that we cherish like a blade through flesh, we have a promise no weapon can touch: the Lord will provide. He will, because it's who he is. He will, because in Christ he's done so already.

5

Our Father in Heaven

See what kind of love the Father has given to us, that
we should be called children of God; and so we are.

1 JOHN 3:1

NEONATAL ICUS ARE otherworldly places.

Adult and even pediatric ICUs hum with activity. Teams of
doctors flow into and out of rooms in tides, murmuring as they
go. Nurses call to each other for help in turning a patient. Awake
patients cry out for ice cubes or pain relief, and even those asleep
cough against the tubes in their throats, triggering their ventilators
to trumpet in protest.

By contrast, the atmosphere of a neonatal ICU (NICU), where
premature babies wait until they can handle the world, is hushed.
The same monitors display heart tracings on the walls. Machinery
and medications still support breathing and blood pressure. Yet
the activity unfolds in quiet motions, without the harried pace of
other ICUs.

The quietness reflects, in part, our instinct to tread with gentle
footfalls among sleeping infants. Yet when we enter the halls of a

NICU, we also step softly because we sense the fragility of its oc-
cupants—their lungs still just buds, their immune systems unripe.
The youngest people in the hospital, some just hours old, most
unprepared to quit the womb, nestle in incubators that look more
like aquariums than cradles and that stand like tiny islands in rooms
meant to accommodate adult-sized machinery.

Parents become acquainted with their children in bittersweet
moments in this grave quietness. Mothers sit beside the incubators
singing rhymes and reading picture books. Occasionally they'll be
allowed to duck a hand into the incubator to stroke a tender scalp,
or to moisten lips curved around a breathing tube like opening
petals. In these mothers' eyes you can see the longing, the yearning
to hold the little ones who once fluttered and turned within them.

A father's posture in the NICU varies. Many stand with an arm
wrapped around their wives to shield them from further injury.
Others hang toward the back of the room, arms folded as they si-
lently process each confusing detail. Still more gaze past the tangle
of catheters and cords to joke about their baby's wrinkled hands,
surely fashioned for the big leagues.

Common to all is a complex web of emotions. Parents breathe
with relief that medicine has sustained their babies, but then shake
their heads at the backwardness of it all. The emptiness of their
arms seems perverse. Everything, it seems, has gone wrong, the
order of the world turned inside out.

There is a breed of tragedy especially reserved for places like
these, where disease dampens the blush of childhood. When I
would examine such babies during my training, using a single
gloved finger to feel for a hernia or a painful belly, I would wonder about the lives these tiny people would lead, who they would
become, whom they would love. Then, in a moment of realism

I hated to acknowledge, I'd pray they'd leave the unit to live out those days. In this way, pediatric illness offers a glimpse of sin at its most malevolent. Sin corrupts what is by nature good, vulnerable, and beautiful.

And yet, even amidst the sadness, in the silent halls of the NICU we can discern echoes of God's love.

I glimpsed such a reflection in Jim. A bricklayer by trade, he filled every room he entered, his frame crowding out walls and doorjambs. When his infant son was born premature and in crisis, Jim aimed to be his family's rock. He cavorted with his daughter when his wife needed time alone to cry. He joked when she needed to laugh. He asked questions when words failed her.

One evening, I found him alone beside his son's incubator. His crouched position looked uncomfortable, especially for someone of his girth.

"Hey, bud, Dr. Katie's here," he told his baby boy when I entered the room. He glanced up, and forced a smile. "He's been holding on to me a lot these days. His little heart's been through so much, but he's still so strong."

I peered into the incubator. His son, fast asleep, had wrapped his entire hand around Jim's gloved index finger.

"You stay strong, buddy," he whispered. "You hold onto me as much as you want. I'm not ever letting you go."

Fatherly Love

Some view biblical descriptions of God as our Father as a stumbling block. This side of the fall, with sin staining each of us, earthly fathers fall short of God's glory (Rom. 3:23). Some berate or demean their children. Others offer coldness instead of affection, or absence when their kids most need guidance. In the worst cases, fathers turn violent. When we look to such dads to understand our heavenly Father, we may see only wrath, aloofness, or tyranny, and so we can't comprehend the attributes of love and faithfulness of which the Bible speaks.

As much as our experiences influence us, when we judge God by the actions of his creation, we approach him backward. God makes man in his image, not the other way around. When our fathers fail us, that failure points not to God, but to the power of sin to creep into our every thought, word, and deed.

Only when we witness fatherhood at its *best*—when dads sacrifice for their families, carry their children through bruised knees and broken hearts, and hold tight to their infants—does it hint of our true Father in heaven. Virtues in fatherhood are the overflow of our heavenly Father's love for his own Son, which has flourished since before the universe began: "In the beginning was the Word, and the Word was with God, and the Word was God" (John 1:1). During Jesus's baptism, heaven opened up and the Father declared, "You are my beloved Son; with you I am well pleased" (Luke 3:22). The Greek word for "beloved" here is *agapetos*. Unlike the romantic love that weakens the knees, or the brotherly love between peers, the Father loves his Son with *agape* love, a covenantal, unchanging, self-sacrificing love to endure forever.

The astonishing good news for us is that, through Jesus's resurrection, *we too are God's beloved children.* The same eternal love that radiates between the heavenly Father and the Son also pours out upon us. Jesus prays about this adoption of his disciples in his high priestly prayer:

> The glory that you have given me I have given to them, that they may be one even as we are one, I in them and you in me,

that they may become perfectly one, so that the world may know that you sent me and loved them even as you loved me. Father, I desire that they also, whom you have given me, may be with me where I am, to see my glory that you have given me because you loved me before the foundation of the world. . . . I made known to them your name, and I will continue to make it known, that the love with which you have loved me may be in them, and I in them. (John 17:22–24, 26)

Paul further elaborates on our divine adoption in his letter to the Ephesians: "In love he predestined us for adoption to himself as sons through Jesus Christ, according to the purpose of his will, to the praise of his glorious grace, with which he has blessed us in the Beloved" (Eph. 1:4–6). In Romans Paul writes, "For all who are led by the Spirit of God are sons of God. For you did not receive the spirit of slavery to fall back into fear, but you have received the Spirit of adoption as sons, by whom we cry, 'Abba! Father!'" (Rom. 8:14–15). John, too, rejoices at our magnificent gift: "See what kind of love the Father has given to us, that we should be called children of God; and so we are" (1 John 3:1).

Think about how amazing this is! When we call God our Father, we don't refer to the broken examples of fatherhood that riddle the here and now. Rather, we acknowledge that through Christ, *God has adopted us as his beloved children.* Through Christ, the heavenly Father extends to us the love he has shared with the Son for all eternity. This Father will never abandon us. He is never haughty, never vindictive or cruel. He remains steadfast in his love for us even when we turn from him. As the parable of the prodigal son reveals, when we plead for forgiveness, he doesn't rebuke or demean us. Instead, he *runs* to us: "But while he was still a long way off, his father saw him and felt compassion, and ran and embraced him and kissed him" (Luke 15:20). Our Father treasures us with such a radical, perfect love that he searches the horizon for us when we've strayed. And when we return, he rushes to enfold us, to welcome us to our true home, in communion with him.

We were once dead in our sins and trespasses (Eph. 2:1). Like infants too feeble for this world, we reached and grasped, but could not pull ourselves to a stand.

As we strained and flailed, through Christ our Father reached down and held us. While we thrashed, he extended a steady hand.

While our own fathers may disappoint us, or fall short, or hurt us, we have a Father in heaven, Lord over all, who will never fail us (Matt. 5:48). Sin bears down. Illness and loss buffet us like a twisting wind. But in Christ, God reaches down to where we lie helpless and flaccid, and takes hold of us. As a loving Father to his children, he takes hold and never lets go.

6

Man Shall Not Live by Bread Alone

*It is written, "Man shall not live by bread alone, but
by every word that comes from the mouth of God."*

MATTHEW 4:4

"ROOM 219. BRING KFC. Dark meat."

"Does that mean you've been admitted?"

"Just hurry. I swear they're trying to kill me with this food!"

An hour later, our family arrived in David's hospital room with his requested bucket of Kentucky Fried drumsticks. He'd been admitted with trouble breathing again. Thankfully, after a night of aerosolized medicines and additional oxygen, he'd regained both ease of breathing and his sense of humor.

"David, is this okay?" I asked as we entered, holding the bucket aloft but eyeing him doubtfully. "There's loads of salt in this. Are you on a restricted diet?"

"Yeah. Flavor restricted!"

Groaning for Nourishment

Hospitals aren't known for their cuisine. During my surgical training, our cafeteria was kind enough to offer a free meal at nine o'clock in the evening to trainees working at the hospital overnight. At 8:45 a line of disheveled and weary young doctors reliably snaked around the serving counter, pagers at our hips, Styrofoam plates in hand.

As overworked and underpaid trainees, we were thankful for free food, but after hours spent sitting on a warmer, every dish congealed into a singular gooey consistency. Mashed potatoes, mashed squash, graying mashed peas, mushy meatloaf in gravy with a thickened skin—it all melded together. We didn't so much swallow it, as let it slither down the throat. As I'd choke the stuff down in my call room, my thoughts would turn to my patients, ill and homesick, who waited all day for these meals to arrive under plastic lids. A pang of pity would stab me.

Whatever the circumstances, hospital food seems guaranteed to spark a longing for homemade cooking. We lift the cover from a plate of unrecognizable meat, wrinkle our noses, and pine for the favorite meals of holidays, when family and warmth and the satisfaction of a full belly abound. Those of us on restricted diets yearn for the freedom to add a dash of salt to lift the flavor, a dollop of butter to smoothen the texture. We wonder if getting better is worth forsaking the simple joy of good food around a table.

For some of us, the longing turns earnest. Perhaps, due to infection or cancer smoldering within, we're disallowed to eat at all. Our lips soon chap, our tongues fissure. Our abdomens distend and echo like drums, while our limbs waste away, sacrificing their own muscle tissue to feed our starving bodies.

For others, nausea turns the very thought of food repugnant. For still more, reveries of warm drinks and steaming meals taunt continually. If sickness plagues us long term, we may rely upon feedings through a tube to sustain us, and daily we groan as a canister of formula the color of wet clay, bearing no resemblance to the roast chicken or spaghetti we crave, masquerades as our nourishment.

In this strange state, when we're sustained but never really fed, bitterness sets in. When we're deprived of something as fundamental as food and drink, soon we doubt other things we once took for granted: who we are, where we're headed. Who God is. Whether he's good.

Consider the Israelites in the wilderness, how quickly their praises turned to groanings once their bellies started to grumble. The moment hunger announced itself, they forgot everything God had done for them during the exodus: the frogs, the Nile, the Passover, the parting seas (Ex. 7–14). In one moment, all the women danced with tambourines to proclaim God's greatness (Ex. 15:20–21). In the next, they whined and moaned about their vacant stomachs, and would gladly have traded their divinely won freedom for a pot of meat (Ex. 16:3). Hunger so consumes us that in a state of lightheadedness we can focus on little else but its steady gnaw.

Not by Bread Alone

Throughout the Bible, we see that God feeds his children. His provision began in the garden, where he offered Adam and Eve every lush plant for food (Gen. 2:9). When they rebelled, hunger crept into the bellies of mankind, and the ground yielded sustenance only when worked (Gen. 3:18–19). Still, God fed his people. He drew Joseph out of slavery to feed the Israelites during famine (Gen. 50:20). He commissioned ravens to bring Elijah bread and meat when drought scorched the land (1 Kings 17:6), and miraculously lengthened the supply of oil and flour for the widow of Zarephath (1 Kings 17:16). When his people cried out for food in the desert, he provided: "Yet he commanded the skies above / and opened the doors of heaven, / and he rained down on them manna to eat / and gave them the grain of heaven. / Man ate of the bread of the angels; / he sent them food in abundance" (Ps. 78:23–25). Jesus reminds us that as a father provides nourishment for his family, so also our Father in heaven satisfies our spiritual hunger when we beseech him in faith: "What father among you, if his son asks for a fish, will instead of a fish give him a serpent; or if he asks for an egg, will give him a scorpion? If you, then, who are evil, know how to give good gifts to your children, how much more will the heavenly Father give the Holy Spirit to those who ask him!" (Luke 11:11–13).

Note Jesus's qualifier in verse 13: "to those who ask him." Our hunger has a purpose. Our Father longs to give us good gifts, but the most exquisite gift of all is our relationship with him. When the pangs twist our stomachs, they're to turn us toward God, the one who satisfies our most strident longings.

Moses described this purpose in the book of Deuteronomy. With his own death inching close and God's promise to deliver the Israelites to Canaan soon to be fulfilled, Moses urged his people to remember God's provision for them: "And he humbled you and let you hunger and fed you with manna, which you did not know, nor did your fathers know, that he might make you know that man does not live by bread alone, but man lives by every word that comes from the mouth of the LORD" (Deut. 8:3). God allowed hunger to unsettle his people, and then frosted the grass with manna and glutted the sky with meat so they would know that trust in him is the ultimate nourishment. When our mouths parch and our stomachs groan, we're to remember Proverbs 3:5: "Trust in the LORD with all your heart, and do not lean on your own understanding."

Lest we dismiss Moses's urging as a poetic gesture, consider that Jesus used his same words *to defeat Satan*. In the wilderness, when Satan tempted Jesus to command stones to morph into bread, the Son of God countered with Deuteronomy 8:3: "It is written, 'Man shall not live by bread alone, but by every word that comes from the mouth of God'" (Matt. 4:4). In refuting the adversary in this way, Jesus revealed himself to be the true Israel, who turned to God's word rather than to earthly idols in times of need. He offered the response we all should voice, but which in our sinful state we never do. He illustrated that even as our limbs atrophy, God can satisfy our most profound hungers. When we rely upon him rather than on our own limited hands, we strip Satan of his power.

God is the one who designed our bodies such that the pleasure of a steaming plate also supplies the crucial molecules our cells need. He's the one who provides every morsel and husk of grain we savor.

God is also the only one who can quell the brittle hunger of our souls.

The Bread of Life

While redeemed, we remain fallen in sin. When the hollowness growls in our bellies, like the Israelites in the desert we grumble. We long for sweetness and salt, and grow bitter with the lack. When we should yearn for God, we dream only of bread.

Still, God feeds us. He doesn't strand us with our hunger. We wail, and yearn, and complain, and through Christ he still provides for us. "For if, because of one man's trespass, death reigned through that one man, much more will those who receive the abundance of grace and the free gift of righteousness reign in life through the one man Jesus Christ" (Rom. 5:17). When we cannot feed ourselves, and when with our stiff necks we dream not of God but of food that tomorrow will rot, God still feeds us.

Through Christ, God fills us with grace that no coveted meal could deliver. "I am the bread of life," Jesus says. "Whoever comes to me shall not hunger, and whoever believes in me shall never thirst" (John 6:35). He further promises: "I am the living bread that came down from heaven. If anyone eats of this bread, he will live forever. And the bread that I give for the life of the world is my flesh" (John 6:51). Christ laid down his life for us, that our souls might be satisfied forever. In him, we find sustenance to quiet the most desperate longings within our souls.

When a nurse unveils yet another canister of tube feed formula, or when we yearn for a favorite meal or scoff at hospital food devoid of flavor, we can remember the bread of life. Hunger makes us faint. But in Christ, we have the promise of bread that chases away our yearnings for all eternity.

Father God, let my hunger raise my eyes to you. Let me know, to my depths, that while pangs trouble me now, Jesus Christ is the bread of life. Through his sacrifice and resurrection, you offer me sustenance that will satisfy my soul forever. In Jesus's name may we pray. Amen.

7

Blessed Be the Name of the Lord

The LORD gave, and the LORD has taken
away; blessed be the name of the LORD.

JOB 1:21

THE MOST GRAVELY ILL person ever entrusted to my care was a young man. He was healthy until he developed an inflamed appendix, one of the most routine problems a surgeon encounters. I met him because, while he awaited surgery, something nonroutine occurred: he threw up, accidentally inhaled some of the vomit, and became horribly sick.

Intestinal contents churn with enzymes, and the acid within stomach fluid is strong enough to corrode metal.[1] When this concoction encounters delicate lung tissue, it burns the lungs, triggers the immune system, and lays the groundwork for pneumonia. Anyone who suffers such an "aspiration event" can require an ICU stay with a breathing machine and blood pressure support for at least a few days, longer if pneumonia develops.

---

1   Winifred Rebhandl et al., "In Vitro Study of Ingested Coins: Leave Them or Retrieve Them?," *Journal of Pediatric Surgery* 42 no. 10 (2007): 1729–34.

Those of us who received this young man in the ICU knew how to manage aspiration. We expected him to worsen over the next forty-eight hours, and knew to scrutinize his ventilator settings and to carefully balance his need for fluid against the risk of further flooding his lungs.

None of us, however, expected him to suffer the most massive inflammatory reaction we'd ever seen.

The lung injury provoked his immune system into overdrive. Every capillary in his body dilated and leaked. His blood pressure plummeted. With the barriers between capillary and tissue disrupted, fluid saturated his lungs, and his oxygen levels sank. For a full two hours, in an ICU of nineteen other critically ill patients, I couldn't step away from his bedside.

We restored his blood pressure with high doses of medication, but despite all our efforts, we couldn't help his lungs. Although we'd adjusted his ventilator settings to the maximum support he could tolerate, turned him over in the bed, and paralyzed him to relax his chest muscles, his oxygen levels still hovered at a level incompatible with life. The respiratory therapist, who'd stood beside me continuously working with the ventilator, finally dropped his arms in defeat. "I don't know where to go from here," he said.

We couldn't keep him alive with the usual measures, so we took an extreme one: we called for a specialist to place him on a lung bypass machine. Extracorporeal membrane oxygenation (ECMO) replaces the function of diseased lungs by diverting blood to an apparatus that adds oxygen and removes carbon dioxide. It requires the surgical placement of two large catheters, chemical thinning of the blood to prevent clotting within the circuit,[2] and continu-

---

2   The most recent circuits no longer require a blood thinner.

ous monitoring. *Please, God, let this work*, I prayed as technicians started the system.

On ECMO, his oxygen levels improved, but he still required astronomical doses of medications to keep him alive. His blood pressure dipped so low that every minute he required adrenaline at doses normally reserved for cardiac arrest. When our hospital's stock of adrenaline dwindled, the pharmacy appealed to the state, who warned us that we risked depleting supplies statewide.

Meanwhile, over the next few days we met repeatedly with his family. The ordeal stunned his parents, who spent our conversations either in pleading inquiry, or in reminiscence, as if they expected him to return home the following day. They especially worried for his disabled daughter, who was wheelchair bound and dependent upon his care. "I don't know what she'll do without him," his mother would say. And then, over and over, "He just *has* to get better. He *has* to."

For a week, his immune system churned a storm in his body. The high doses of medications ultimately blackened his fingers and toes. Still, chest X-rays suggested his lungs were starting to clear, and we hoped that with the ECMO he might turn the corner.

Then, one morning, his nurse made a horrifying discovery. One of his pupils had tripled its size, and didn't respond to light.

Dread compelled us into silence as a portable CT scanner hummed past the arsenal of machinery sustaining him. The images of his brain confirmed our fears: the blood thinner used in the ECMO circuit had caused massive cerebral hemorrhage.[3] After so many heroic measures and so many prayers, one of medical science's

---

3 This event occurred about a decade ago. The prior risk of bleeding on ECMO has recently prompted development of circuits that run without blood thinners.

most sophisticated treatments—the best we had to offer—had delivered a fatal blow.

The news broke his parents. For fifteen minutes his father shouted, cursing us, the team in the operating room, the emergency department physicians, his son's employer, anyone on whom he could pin a modicum of responsibility. His mother sat beside him quivering like a reed in the wind, rocking back and forth and crying, "This can't be happening," over and over. I watched the heartbreak unfold, felt my chest tighten, and searched my mind for the right words. Nothing I could say could mend this wound. Nothing could turn back the hands of time to undo all the harrowing and ultimately futile events of the past week. "I'm so sorry," was all I could stammer.

It was so horribly insufficient. The patient's father just glared at me, and I understood why.

We'd hoped to continue the patient's medical support for several hours, to give all family members time to say goodbye, but when we returned to his bedside after the meeting his heart rate dived low. I raced back to the conference room, and found his parents holding each other.

"We don't have much time," I said.

His mother began to cry again, and tears finally broke through his father's anger. "His daughter needs to be here," he insisted.

Half an hour later, while we pushed medications to prod on his heart, his daughter appeared outside his room. Her legs, limp in her wheelchair, had shriveled long ago, and her contracted arms angled across her chest. Reddened eyes betrayed the recent tears someone had wiped clean before her arrival. Her grandfather's face, so severe during discussions with us, softened at the sight of her.

"She won't be able to see him in that chair, it's not high enough," he said. He glanced at his son's hospital bed, which we'd elevated several feet higher than normal to accommodate the ECMO. "Is there something you can do, so she can see his face?"

A team of nurses lifted her onto a stretcher. They moved aside monitors to create a pathway, then wheeled her into the room so she could lie alongside her father. She couldn't reach across the expanse between stretcher and hospital bed because her arms, long immobile, had locked into flexion. Instead, she gazed upon the face she still recognized despite the tubes, lines, and swelling of sickness. "I love you, Daddy," she said.

The nurse burst into tears, and I turned to the wall to hide my own. *God, this is too much,* I prayed. *Please, can't you heal this?* I knew the Lord works all things for good for those who love him (Rom. 8:28). But what good could come of a disabled girl orphaned when she couldn't care for herself? What beauty manifested, after a week of heroic efforts, in a man's life cut off, his death sped by the very measures meant to save him?

A few minutes later, his heart, which had endured so much, finally surrendered. Alarms sounded. I listened to his chest with a stethoscope to confirm the silence within, and his mother shut her eyes and wept. His daughter howled. His father broke down. As I ducked from the room, I prayed that somehow, in some way we couldn't see, God would engage with the wreckage for good.

Questions That Haunt

We've already seen that the Lord provides. Jesus himself encourages us not to worry about food or clothing, because God will attend to our needs:

> Consider the lilies of the field, how they grow: they neither toil nor
> spin, yet I tell you, even Solomon in all his glory was not arrayed

like one of these. But if God so clothes the grass of the field, which today is alive and tomorrow is thrown into the oven, will he not much more clothe you, O you of little faith? (Matt. 6:28–30)

Lest we doubt, we need only cast our gaze upon the cross to rediscover God's provision for us, given out of grace (Eph. 2:1–7).

Yet in life's worst moments, signs of God's provision can elude us. We search our surroundings for the sacrificial ram, the appointed fish, or the bread from heaven, but find only devastation. We stand at the bedside of a young man, loved and needed, watch his daughter cry for him, and wonder, *Lord, what are you doing? How can this possibly be right?*

Euphemisms fail in such moments, with good reason. If simple answers to our worst quandaries abounded, we could manage sin on our own, and wouldn't need a Savior. We need God's grace precisely because we can't shrug off the evils that ravage the world.

And yet, God so loves us that he doesn't leave us completely adrift. His Scripture includes a narrative that offers insight when disaster strikes: the book of Job.

Trouble Comes

Job was a contemporary of the patriarchs, "blameless and upright, one who feared God and turned away from evil" (Job 1:1). The Hebrew word for "blameless" in this context doesn't denote sinlessness, but rather integrity (Josh. 24:14). Job's fear of God echoes Proverbs 1:7: "The fear of the LORD is the beginning of knowledge; / fools despise wisdom and instruction." Job, then, was both righteous and wise, a faithful servant who so honored God that he offered sacrifices to atone for the sins his children might have committed "in their hearts" (Job 1:5).

Despite his devotion to the Lord, within the very first chapter Job's life imploded. His livestock were slaughtered or stolen. Enemies murdered his servants. Every one of his children died in a natural disaster. In a last calamity, painful sores afflicted Job from head to foot. His every treasured possession and loved one destroyed, his body wretched, Job could do nothing but sit in the ashes and scrape himself with shards of pottery (Job 2:8).

Job's response to such loss is arresting. First, Job tore his robe and shaved his head, both traditional signs of mourning (Job 1:20). We can all relate to that reaction, the flood of anguish, the tears. However, he then did something surprising: he fell to the ground and *worshiped*. "Naked I came from my mother's womb, and naked shall I return," he said. "The LORD gave, and the LORD has taken away; blessed be the name of the LORD" (Job 1:21).

Every earthly thing Job prized had vanished. The children he adored were gone, their names and faces and the rise of their laughter alive in his memory only. And yet in the midst of his grief, Job still clung to God, even *praised* him.

Job's remarkable intertwining of lamentation with worship continues throughout the book. In chapter 3, Job cursed the day of his birth in verses that echo the Psalms:

For my sighing comes instead of my bread,
    and my groanings are poured out like water.
For the thing that I fear comes upon me,
    and what I dread befalls me.
I am not at ease, nor am I quiet;
    I have no rest, but trouble comes. (Job 3:24–26)

For the next thirty chapters, he debated with "miserable comforters" who hurt more than helped him, and his prayers evolved into complaints: "Why have you made me your mark? / Why have I become a burden to you? / Why do you not pardon my transgression / and take away my iniquity?" (Job 7:20–21). As companions barraged him with accusations of wrongdoing, Job's confidence faltered, and his prayers grew more desperate. But he never denounced God. Job lamented, yearned to understand, protested, and even harangued God for answers, but he never denied who God is: the author of the earth, "who does great things beyond searching out, and marvelous things beyond number" (Job 9:10).

Job's response reveals to us that deep grief, the type that wells up from within and abrades the heart raw, is an appropriate response to suffering. We were not created for a sinful world, and tragedies rightfully earn our tears. Even Jesus, kneeling in a garden on the eve of his execution, was "sorrowful, even to death" (Matt. 26:38): "And being in agony he prayed more earnestly; and his sweat became like great drops of blood falling down to the ground" (Luke 22:44).

Job also teaches us that our afflictions, however severe, *don't diminish God's character*. Whether we flourish or suffer, *God remains who he is*. His goodness, mercy, holiness, sovereignty, steadfastness, and patience don't change.

Whatever sin stirs up on earth, his name remains blessed. Whatever tribulation afflicts us, he remains our hope.

Meaning in Tragedy

God didn't reply to Job's complaints with an explanation that tidily resolved his questions. He didn't satisfy all Job's appeals. Rather, he reminded Job that he created the heavens and the earth, that he commands the weather, subdues chaos, and governs every living thing. In short, he assured Job of *who he is*.

At first blush this response frustrates us. A deep desire to claim God's knowledge for ourselves has stirred within us since the garden (Gen. 3:6). We know that God is sovereign and good, but our sin nature convinces us that *this is not enough*. We yearn for our sufferings to have meaning we can see and hold, turn over and inspect. We want explanations, a window into what God knows.

However earnest our hunger for answers, rarely do we understand the reasons for our sufferings, because we simply cannot fathom the things of God. "For as the heavens are higher than the earth, / so are my ways higher than your ways / and my thoughts than your thoughts," the Lord declares in Isaiah 55:9.

Yet even when we don't comprehend suffering, we learn from Job that *meaning is there*. We learn in the prologue that although Job couldn't discern a purpose in his woes, they paved the way for a triumph more magnificent than he could have ever imagined: victory over the adversary.

Satan wanders the earth seeking to ensnare mankind and to undermine God. In the first chapter of Job, Satan appeared before God and accused Job of insincere faith. "Stretch out your hand and touch all that he has," Satan alleged, "and he will curse you to your face" (Job 1:11). His attack on Job was a challenge to God's power, a claim that God's most righteous servant obeyed out of self-interest rather than devotion. We see in this encounter that Job's afflictions, which God permitted but limited out of mercy (Job 1:12), served a cosmic purpose: the humiliation of the deceiver, who "prowls around like a roaring lion, seeking someone to devour" (1 Pet. 5:8). When Job perseveres through his misery, all the while keeping God's name holy, we envision Satan slinking away in defeat. We learn from Job that our sufferings, too, can have meaning indiscernible with mortal eyes.

At the conclusion of the book, God restores the fortunes of Job, giving him "twice as much as he had before" (Job 42:10), and blessing "the latter days of Job more than his beginning" (Job 42:12). Likewise, while God doesn't promise freedom from suffering in this life, through Christ he guarantees restoration in the new heavens and the new earth (Rev. 21:1–4).

My Redeemer Lives

Job died too soon to witness the Messiah's coming, yet still he leaned upon God's promise of redemption through Christ. We're blessed to know the full story, to stand in the shadow of the cross, where the barrier between sinful man and holy God crumbles. When we linger at the bedside of a dying loved one, or bear the agony of illness ourselves and cannot perceive good in what scourges us, Job's words remind us of that sweet grace:

> For I know that my Redeemer lives,
>   and at the last he will stand upon the earth.
> And after my skin has been thus destroyed,
>   yet in my flesh I shall see God,
> whom I shall see for myself,
>   and my eyes shall behold, and not another. (Job 19:25–27)

There are no easy answers in the face of untimely death. No bandages can cover the hurt of irrevocable loss. Such wounds penetrate too deeply. We can't knit them back together.

We have no easy answers, but we do have assurance. In Christ, God has triumphed over the enemy, and so the afflictions that assail us now will not endure forever. "For this light and momentary affliction is preparing us for an eternal weight of glory beyond all comparison, as we look not to the things that are seen but to the things that are unseen. For the things that are seen are transient, but the things that are unseen are eternal" (2 Cor. 4:17–18).

Amid all the agony, God remains who he is. His love for you endures. His power and his mercy envelop you, even when you cannot see him. And his name remains blessed, even when unspeakable calamities strike, even when sin seems to swallow up the world.

Illness cuts us in two. Sin tears us apart. But our Redeemer lives. Blessed is the name of the Lord.

8

My Grace Is Sufficient

Three times I pleaded with the Lord about this, that it
should leave me. But he said to me, "My grace is sufficient
for you, for my power is made perfect in weakness."

2 CORINTHIANS 12:8–9

WEEKS OF CHEMOTHERAPY eroded the lining of her mouth and mangled her immune system. As she underwent an hours-long surgery to carve a tumor the size of a grapefruit from her belly, friends and loved ones lifted up a heartfelt but singular prayer: *Heal her, Lord.* As she recovered in the hospital with a silicone tube snaking down her nose and throat, she wrapped herself in their words as if nestling into a blanket.[1]

When she returned home, she discovered that food had lost its flavor, and her everyday routines exhausted her. The passing days sapped her strength, and within a few weeks her limbs wasted to skeletal proportions. Then she read a line on the pathology report that mentioned dead cells at the center of the tumor. She rejoiced,

---

1   I first wrote about this patient in "If God Doesn't Heal You," January 27, 2018, desiringGod. org, https://www.desiringgod.org/articles/if-god-doesnt-heal-you.

convinced that the chemotherapy had destroyed the cancer before her surgeon ever put knife to skin. Despite her decline, the report persuaded her that the healing for which she'd prayed was at hand. But those dead cells didn't promise cure. Instead, they indicated a cancer so aggressive that it couldn't support its own middle. It had grown so rapidly that no blood vessels could tunnel to its center.

Months later, the cancer not only returned but spread, clogging her lungs and dotting her brain. As the delicate balance of her organ systems teetered and collapsed, prayers for a cure became more ardent, from her church as well as from her own lips. Her doctors recommended home hospice, but she clung to her conviction that God *must* melt away her disease, and insisted upon last-ditch chemotherapy.

Still, the cancer continued its deadly march. Fluid filled her abdomen and saturated her lungs. One awful night, with ICU alarms sounding her elegy, her heart quivered and stopped.

Her family reeled in grief and shock. They'd shared her conviction that God would melt away her cancer, and couldn't reconcile the flickering out of her life against their continual appeals for cure. How could God dismiss their prayers, when she was so faithful to him? How could her death possibly be the right answer? Had God even listened? Over and against their tears, an unspoken protest simmered: they'd prayed over and over. This wasn't supposed to happen.

Let Your Requests Be Made Known to God

Pleas for healing frequent the prayer lists of every church, and with good reason. All throughout his ministry Jesus performed miraculous healings that glorified the Father and deepened faith (Matt. 4:23; Luke 4:40). God made heaven and earth, and assembled the scaffolding of our cytoplasm. Surely, he can also eradicate cancer, realign our bones, and restore blood flow to areas that mottle. Jesus instructs his disciples, "Therefore I tell you, whatever you ask in prayer, believe that you have received it, and it will be yours" (Mark 11:24). Paul reaffirms, "The Lord is at hand; do not be anxious about anything, but in everything by prayer and supplication with thanksgiving let your requests be made known to God" (Phil. 4:5–6). If the Spirit moves us to pray for healing, whether for ourselves or our neighbors, the Bible guides us to do so with fervor.

And yet, while we may perceive our healing to be the greatest good, *God's wisdom surpasses the farthest reaches of our understanding* (Isa. 55:8).

The chief end of man is not to escape pain or to enjoy long life but, as the Westminster Catechism so elegantly summarizes, "to glorify God, and fully to enjoy him for ever."[2] When viewed against the span of eternity, our relationship with God is far more precious than the transient wellness of our bodies. While God *can* heal us, according to his divine and sovereign wisdom, bodily restoration might not be the greatest good.

To understand this, consider the apostle Paul's words in his second letter to the Corinthians. "A thorn was given me in the flesh . . . ," he writes. "Three times I pleaded with the Lord about this, that it should leave me. But he said to me, 'My grace is sufficient for you, for my power is made perfect in weakness'" (2 Cor. 12:7–9). Paul prays for relief, and in so doing he affirms that prayer for healing is good and right, as fitting as the plea of a child for help from his father. When no help comes, however, Paul doesn't

---

2   Question 1 in *The Larger Catechism of the Westminster Assembly* (Glasgow, Free Presbyterian Publications, 2001), 3.

rail against God or fall into despair. Rather, he discerns God's answer as a means to draw Paul to himself. His pain, the "thorn in the flesh," highlights his need for a Savior, and reminds him that our greatest need is neither deliverance from hurt nor reparation of our bodies, but a renewed relationship with God. His grace is most apparent to us not when we're conquering the world, but rather when we're brought low, stricken and bereft, with nowhere to look but heavenward.

So That You May Believe

The raising of Lazarus provides another vivid example of how God works through tragedy to draw us to himself. When Lazarus fell deathly ill, Martha and Mary pleaded with Jesus to come to his aid. As Jesus had healed multitudes and cared for the masses throughout his ministry, we might expect him to have raced to his ailing friend's side, especially when we learn that Jesus loved Lazarus as a brother (John 11:3).

Yet shockingly, rather than swoop in to rescue his friend from death, Jesus *stalled*. He waited another two days, and embarked on his journey only after Lazarus died. His remark to his disciples en route must have mystified them, perhaps even struck them as callous: "Lazarus has died, and for your sake I am glad that I was not there, so that you may believe" (John 11:14–15).

Martha, grief-stricken, could not fathom his actions. "Lord, if you had been here, my brother would not have died," she lamented (John 11:21).

Yet just like the sufferings of Job, Jesus's delay served a purpose no human could discern.

Jesus joined Mary and others beside the tomb. He wept because he loved Lazarus and because death tears rents in all that is good, true, and lovely. Then he commanded them to roll away the stone sealing the tomb, against Martha's protest that Lazarus's body would have already begun to decay. What happened next is astonishing:

> And Jesus lifted up his eyes and said, "Father, I thank you that you have heard me. I knew that you always hear me, but I said this on account of the people standing around, that they may believe that you sent me." When he had said these things, he cried out with a loud voice, "Lazarus, come out." The man who had died came out, his hands and feet bound with linen strips, and his face wrapped with a cloth. (John 11:41–44)

Now we learn the startling reason for Jesus's delay, the truth apparent to the divine but shielded from the comprehension of men. Jesus allowed Lazarus to die so that he might raise him again, displaying to all his power as the Son of God. He delayed so that those who mourned would witness this miracle, see Jesus, and believe.

At first Jesus seemed to ignore Martha and Mary's pleas for help, a response that must have confused them and even seemed cruel. Yet in the aftermath, we see his delay was for a greater good, and a greater glory, than they could have ever imagined. He still saved Lazarus! And Jesus's initial silence revealed the righteousness of God in brushstrokes more magnificent than simple healing could have accomplished.

As we grapple with the afflictions that seize our own bodies in this life, we may wonder why Jesus delays in rescuing us. *God has the power to heal me*, we think. *So why doesn't he?*

In John 11, we glimpse an answer. We bear God's image, but not his essence. We reflect his goodness as the moon reflects the sunlight, but we can't radiate glory on our own. We can't grasp his mind or duplicate his ways. And so when we pray but hear only silence, it doesn't mean he's ignoring us. When we bid him come and he delays, he hasn't abandoned us. Rather, even when we can't fathom how, in all things God is working "for the good of those who love him" (Rom. 8:28), *so that we might believe.*

This, Then, Is How You Should Pray

How then, if God can heal but doesn't always, do we pray for relief from diseases that wrack our bodies?

We can look to Jesus himself for guidance. In the garden of Gethsemane, Jesus prayed for deliverance from the cross. He prayed not with cool composure, but while prostrate upon the ground, his soul "very sorrowful, even to death" (Matt. 26:38). "Being in agony," Luke writes, "he prayed more earnestly; and his sweat became like great drops of blood falling down to the ground" (Luke 22:44). His divine nature was aligned with God's will, but his human nature couldn't bear the anguish to come: his body bruised and shredded, all of God's wrath unleashed upon him.

Remarkably, even as he pleaded for relief from the oncoming suffering, Jesus still trusted in *who the Father is*: "My Father, if it be possible, let this cup pass from me; nevertheless, *not as I will, but as you will*" (Matt. 26:39). Adam, the father of our sins, reveled in the abundance of God's blessings, yet trusted more in his own eyes than in God's sovereign goodness. In contrast, Jesus—the man Adam should have been—fell to the ground on the eve of a death he didn't deserve, pleaded for escape, yet also trusted wholeheartedly, fully, tenderly, in the Father's everlasting love and wisdom. While Adam coveted, Jesus ceded. While Adam trusted himself, Jesus trusted the Father. While Adam's idolatry condemned us to sin and death, Jesus's submission freed us from death forever. "For if, because of one man's trespass, death reigned through that one man, much more will those who receive the abundance of grace and the free gift of righteousness reign in life through the one man Jesus Christ" (Rom. 5:17).

As Jesus's followers watched him gasping on the cross, horror likely leadening their hearts, they must have assumed God ignored their teacher's prayers for rescue. Why didn't the Father intervene? As Jesus cried out, "My God, my God, why have you forsaken me?" (Matt. 27:46), sorrow must have dragged them to the ground. At the foot of the cross, they could see only death, only the black sprawl of evil. The wages of sin sank its claws into their beloved Master, the only one born of woman who'd never sinned. How could this be God's will?

Like us, they didn't have God's vision. Jesus prayed for deliverance from God's wrath. He prayed his life might be spared. But he also prayed for God's will to be done. That will, so incomprehensible to those who watched the sky blacken and Jesus's blood pour out, imparted upon us the greatest gift of mercy the world has ever known.

In three days, the tomb would be empty and the stone would be rolled away. The risen Lord would greet them, dine with them, and embrace them again (Luke 24:40–42). They would touch the wounds in his hands, and they would rejoice that through Jesus's sacrifice and rising, death itself had come undone.

Healing Only from Christ

God didn't answer my patient's prayers in the way she expected. He didn't ablate her cancer or command the cells to halt their multiplication, telling them, as the seas, to come here and no further (Job 38:11).

Yet God *did* heal her. As a disciple of Christ, her end on earth was by no means *the* end. The cancer remained in her earthly body, but through Christ God accomplished something far greater than healing: he adopted her as his daughter (Eph. 1:5–6; 2 Cor. 6:18). He carried her into his love for all eternity. Through the blood of his one and only Son, he gave up everything to make her new.

God doesn't always answer prayers as we expect. Such moments confuse and hurt us. Like Martha and Mary as they gazed down the road and awaited their Savior, we ask why, and the question twists our hearts.

Thanks be to God, Scripture assures us that even when answers elude us, we can trust in the perfect will of the Father. As Jesus prayed "thy will be done," so too can we trust that God works all things for our good, in ways we won't understand until we enter into his glory. Although we may not see how, he draws near to us when we are brokenhearted (Ps. 34:18). When the thorn tears the flesh, his grace is sufficient, and his power is made perfect in weakness.

9

A Gracious God and Merciful

*I knew that you are a gracious God and merciful, slow to anger
and abounding in steadfast love, and relenting from disaster.*

JONAH 4:2

I WILL NEVER FORGET the first patient I failed.[1]

He groaned with the lightest touch of his abdomen, which felt
like a rock beneath my fingers. "Stop!" he growled. For a moment
his glazed eyes locked with mine, and flashed with disdain.

I backpedaled and stammered an apology. As a naive medical
student, I was eager to help, but loathe to overstep my boundaries.
At the end of my shift in the ER, I mumbled an incoherent story
to my supervising physician, and then skulked out of the hospital.

During my surgery rotation a few months later, a resident
guided me through an exam of a patient with a perforated colon.
When his abdomen, taut with infection, didn't yield beneath my
fingers, the memory of the gentleman in the ER flooded back
and stopped me cold.

---

1 From my article "The Only Freedom from Remorse," May 24, 2018, desiringGod.org,
   https://www.desiringgod.org/articles/the-only-freedom-from-remorse.

I had missed peritonitis.

A disaster within the belly shocks the abdominal muscles into a rigid wall. As I recalled the patient in the ER, I realized that I'd missed an infection oozing among his internal organs like a muddy river, leaching bacteria into his bloodstream every second. Without antibiotics and often emergency surgery, patients with peritonitis develop life-threatening sepsis.

In my ignorance, I'd endangered someone in my care.

Never again, I vowed thereafter. Desperate not to harm someone with another mistake, for years afterward I obsessed over every data point. I awoke in the middle of the night to scour medical records from home. I checked and double-checked every order, every lab result, every turn of a clamp in the operating room.

Yet my compulsiveness couldn't redeem me. No matter how many people I returned home to their families, I was never able to sponge away the stain of my failures: my suture lines that didn't hold, the bleeding I couldn't stop, the infections that swept over wounds I had dressed. The teenage boy who cried, "Help me!" in the trauma bay, before dying with my hands around his heart. The girl who yelled, "You're hurting me!" before a procedure I supervised went horribly wrong. I would awaken in the night, these cries echoing from a dream, and gasp for air. *Lord, please forgive me*, I would whisper, over, and over, and over.

All My Fault

My late-night awakenings are no anomaly. In the hospital, where the stakes are high and the outcomes grave, guilt and remorse are routine.

I remember the mother of a dying teenage girl. When the girl's skin sallowed to mustard color, her mother would massage her hands with jasmine-scented lotion. When her eyes, vacant and bloodshot, darted around the room in delirium, her mother papered the walls with photographs to remind them both of what mattered.

The day this poor girl died, her mom climbed into the hospital bed with her. She wrapped her arms around her, enfolding her daughter in the same warmth she'd known in her first moments on earth. As those of us in the ICU stood by, our hands helpless, our ideas run out, all we could do was bear witness to her grief. Abandoning any pretense of professionalism, we cried along with her.

The day before this tender scene, the mother crumpled into a chair and held her head in her hands. "I keep begging God to take out my heart, to keep it from breaking," she said. "But I don't even know if he's listening anymore." I put a hand on her shoulder, and felt her tremble. "My family says this happened to her because I stopped going to church," she said, barely whispering. "They say God's punishing me. *What if this is all my fault?*"

When the Guilt Overwhelms

Chances are high that you, too, have known deep remorse. The wages of sin is death (Rom. 6:23), and in the hospital, we toil in its preamble. Perhaps you're a loved one caring for the dying. As you cradle a mottled hand, do you wrestle with doubts? Do you wonder if you've made the right decision for your loved one's care? Do memories break through the sterility of the room and haunt you with words you should have said? Words you *shouldn't* have said?

Maybe you lie in a hospital bed and gaze at a bland ceiling. What worries taunt you? While you creep toward the threshold, do you glance back and grimace at the events leading you to this moment? Do you regret conversations, actions, or the way you looked at a loved one?

If you're a provider in the hospital, guilt likely constricts your heart like a vice. The threat of inadvertently hurting people stalks your thoughts. You take personal responsibility for the rise and fall of every data point, and yet patients die despite technology, expediency, and finely tuned protocols. When you lose a patient, you consider your inadequate books, your hands that couldn't deliver—and you despair. You recite your report flatly while the crushing weight of your sin bears down upon you. It's no wonder the physician suicide rate is double that of the general population.[2]

Guilt so strangles us because, this side of the fall, we can't redeem ourselves. As Paul writes in Romans 7:19, "For I do not do the good I want, but the evil I do not want is what I keep on doing." This problem of our sin nature snaps into sharp relief in the hospital, where grief and tragedy abound, yet where few converse in a language of atonement. We witness evil, cower from our guilt, and search the halls for forgiveness, but find only white coats, monitors, and more questions in the dark. We study our hands, scrub them, and can't scour away our errors. Unable to work out our own redemption, we bear the guilt.

Yet our Father is "merciful and gracious, slow to anger and abounding in steadfast love" (Ps. 103:8). While we groan under the heft of our remorse, we can also rejoice that Christ removes our transgressions from us as far as the east diverges from the west (Ps. 103:12).

God is holy. God "will by no means clear the guilty" (Ex. 34:7). He is just, perfect, and will not abide evil (Ps. 5:4).

---

2 Omotola T'Sarumi, Anwar Ashraf, and Deepika Tanwar, "Physician Suicide: A Silent Epidemic," *Annual Meeting of the American Psychiatric Association (APA)* (New York: 2018), 1–227.

Yet God is also merciful. And in his mercy, when we profess faith in his Son and confess our sins, "he is faithful and just to forgive us our sins and to cleanse us from all unrighteousness" (1 John 1:9).

A Gracious God and Merciful

The book of Jonah is a spectacular revelation of God's mercy. I love to teach Jonah to young adults, who after a sticky sweet diet of cartoonish Bibles are surprised to learn there's so much more to this story than a big fish. As they dive into the text with mature eyes, God's mercy—toward Jonah, toward the sailors, toward the Ninevites, toward *us*—sings from the pages.

Among prophets in the Bible, Jonah was delinquent. God commissioned him to preach the word to the people, for their good and the Lord's glory. Obedience to God should have been a given. Yet when God called upon Jonah to preach repentance to the Ninevites, an enemy people, he *ran* from God. He fled to Tarshish, 2,500 miles across the Mediterranean Sea, in the exact *opposite* direction of Nineveh.

This was utter tomfoolery. As a prophet, Jonah would have been well versed in the Law and the Psalms, all which clearly teach that no one can hide from God: "Where shall I go from your Spirit? / Or where can I flee from your presence? / If I ascend to heaven, you are there! / If I make my bed in Sheol, you are there!" (Ps. 139:7–8).

Jonah's problem, as is so often the case, was idolatry. We learn in 2 Kings 14 that Jonah was a patriot who played a key role in the expansion of Israel's territory (2 Kings 14:25). On the ship to Tarshish, he identified himself first and foremost by his heritage, and then only secondarily by his relationship to God: "I am a Hebrew, and I fear the Lord, the God of heaven, who made the sea and the dry land" (Jonah 1:9). Swollen with national pride,

Jonah fled from God because he decided the Ninevites didn't deserve a chance to repent. He relished vengeance more than God's wisdom and mercy.

The Ninevites were a brutal people who tortured and enslaved captives of war. Jonah was right: they *didn't* deserve forgiveness. But then, *neither did Jonah*. His brazen defiance placed him squarely under God's wrath. We see as the story unfolds that God extended mercy to *both* these undeserving parties.

God sent a storm to thwart Jonah's retreat. Jonah, rather than repent, hid below deck and fell asleep, endangering the lives of the entire crew. The text tells us that in the midst of the tempest, "the ship threatened to break up" (Jonah 1:4). *Threatened to*, but didn't. God commanded the gale to stop the ship, but not destroy it. Out of mercy.

When Jonah finally dove into the sea, the oceans ceased their frothing. The raging winds settled, and God spared the lives of all on board. Again, out of mercy.

Jonah drifted in the vast waters. He'd run from God, expelling his Creator from the rightful place of honor in his heart. For his rebellion, Jonah deserved to sink into a watery grave.

But God saw Jonah, and had mercy on him. He appointed a fish to swallow him, and in three days, restored him to dry land, just as in three days the Father raised the Son from the tomb, restoring him to life and saving us all (Matt. 12:38–41).

Still, the tide of mercy continued. God repeated his command to Jonah, and this time, the prophet begrudgingly complied. Jonah anticipated three days of preaching, but after just one day, the king of Nineveh commanded all his people to repent. In response, God showed them mercy: "When God saw what they did, how they turned from their evil way, God relented of the disaster that he had said he would do to them, and he did not do it" (Jonah 3:10).

To end the book of Jonah here, when the Ninevites repented, would have concluded the story tidily. All seemed put to right. But a dialogue continues that highlights God's abundant compassion, contrasted with our own tendency toward vindictiveness.

God had poured out mercy like water, but Jonah didn't seem to notice. Instead, he had a temper tantrum. Resentful over Nineveh's escape, he climbed to an overlook and awaited the punishment he was convinced they deserved.

In yet *another* act of mercy, God appointed a plant to shield Jonah from the scorching heat. Again, dismissing God's grace, Jonah reacted with rage when the vine wilted the following day: "I do well to be angry, angry enough to die" (Jonah 4:9).

God's reply to Jonah is astounding:

> You pity the plant, for which you did not labor, nor did you make it grow, which came into being in a night and perished in a night. And should not I pity Nineveh, that great city, in which there are more than 120,000 persons who do not know their right hand from their left, and also much cattle? (Jonah 4:10–11)

This question concludes the chapter, without a response. God's words hang in the air, unanswered, pressing upon us, because God asks it not only of Jonah, but of *us*. Shouldn't God be concerned with his creation?

Do we not know who he is?

God reveals to Jonah, and to us, that he cares for all his creation, from vines that shrivel in an evening, to people and animals that flourish within strongholds. As a father nurtures his children, so our Father loves us, and longs for us to return to him, "not wishing that any should perish, but that all should reach repentance" (2 Pet. 3:9). When we flail in our sin, whether amid storms of our own making or those imposed upon us, according to his mercy he delivers us to dry land, and guides us back into his loving embrace.

God is holy, but he is also merciful. And he is also eager to forgive us.

God appointed Jonah to save the Ninevites, and a fish to save Jonah. So also, he appointed his one and only Son, whom he loved, to reside in the belly of the earth for three days, to redeem you and me from our sins and to gather us into his glorious presence forever. Our failings lash us with guilt and deform our hands. We stand condemned in our trespasses. Yet through the cross, he removes the filthy rags with which we cover our guilt. He washes us clean and clothes us in Christ (Isa. 64:6; Gal. 3:26–27). He carries us through the storm, shelters us, and calls us home to him.

You Brought Up My Life from the Pit

When memories of mistakes you've made, people you've hurt, and lives you've damaged with words, scalpel, or syringe storm you with guilt, remember Jonah flailing in the sea.

When your loved one's eyes close before you've said all you must, and remorse throbs within you, remember how God held back the raging waves from Jonah's boat.

As you worry the stiff hospital sheet beneath you in the sterile dark, and regrets stir you to uneasy wakefulness, recall how God forgave even the brutal Ninevites when they repented. Remember Jonah's prayer while imprisoned within the murk of the fish:

The waters closed in over me to take my life;
the deep surrounded me;

weeds were wrapped about my head
   at the roots of the mountains.
I went down to the land
   whose bars closed upon me forever;
yet you brought up my life from the pit,
   O LORD my God. (Jonah 2:5–6)

Above all, when the blemishes upon your hands will not scrape away and you languish beneath the weight of your sins, remember the sign of Jonah: "For just as Jonah was three days and three nights in the belly of the great fish, so will the Son of Man be three days and three nights in the heart of the earth. . . . And behold, something greater than Jonah is here" (Matt. 12:40–41).

Sin plunges us into a pit from which we cannot escape. Guilt swallows us whole. But God does not abandon us in those depths. In Christ, "he has delivered us from the domain of darkness and transferred us to the kingdom of his beloved Son, in whom we have redemption, the forgiveness of sins" (Col. 1:13–14). Ours is a gracious God, and merciful. And in Christ, we are forgiven.

10

Life and Breath

He himself gives to all mankind life and breath and everything.

ACTS 17:25

In the Garden

The story of mankind began with a breath.

In the beginning, God rolled back the waters of the earth, chiseled the mountains high, and prodded the soil to burst with bloom. He cast birds like fistfuls of gems into the sky.

Then, after surveying all he had made, he crafted the pinnacle of his creation: "Then the LORD God formed the man of dust from the ground and breathed into his nostrils the breath of life, and the man became a living creature" (Gen. 2:7). Once infused with God's breath, Adam was to steward everything that crept and crawled, every flutter of wings, every leaf that curled. He would walk with God in the cool of the day as one beloved. Made in God's image, his descendants would populate the earth with echoes of God's goodness, majesty, and steadfast love.

All with a breath.

In the Delivery Room

Our personal stories also start with a breath.

Our lungs lie quiescent for the duration of our residence in the womb. The heart jolts into action months before we're born. Before the second trimester ends, our brains already house *billions* of neurons, their connections rapidly weaving together.[1] But while blood surges through our lungs, they hang limp in our chests, fluid filling their air spaces.

Not until we emerge ruddy and swollen into the air do our lungs billow into service. We gasp, maybe from the shock of light and cold, maybe from the vigorous rub of a doctor's hand. Our lungs inflate, and that first breath *changes* our circulatory system. The arteries dilate to usher in blood, and a hole in the upper chambers of the heart seals up. With a breath, we transition from an isolated, watery realm into the world God entrusts to us. Our parents weep with joy and relief as we declare our arrival with a gurgling cry: "I am here. I am made in God's image, and I am loved."

In the World

God designed us such that we breathe up to sixteen times per minute—960 times an hour, 23,040 times a day, 8,409,600 times a year—without conscious effort. While we busy our minds with preparing dinner, balancing a budget, or playing soccer with the kids, the respiratory center deep in our brainstem measures carbon dioxide in our bloodstream and triggers a breath when its levels rise. That respiratory center then signals our diaphragm,

---

1 Marion I. van den Heuvel and Moriah E. Thomason, "Functional Connectivity of the Human Brain *in Utero*," *Trends in Cognitive Science* 20 no 12 (2016): 931–39.

a large sheet of muscle dividing the chest from the abdomen, to lower. Our ribs swing outward, and we draw a breath in one fluid movement.

As our lungs expand, the pressure in our airways rises until the flow slows and stops. Oxygen diffuses into and carbon dioxide out of millions of capillaries just a single cell thick. Then our chest wall and diaphragm relax, the way a rubber band recoils into its original form after stretching. Air rich in carbon dioxide rushes back out through our airways. As we pile our kids into the car, the process repeats all over again, all without our bidding.

For most of our lives we breathe unknowingly, although certain moments can heighten our awareness of breathing. We inhale deeply on a brisk autumn morning, when the air feels crisp and bracing. When stressed, we focus on the rise and fall of our chest to regain composure. We purse our lips and pace our breathing as we run. We control it to sing hymns, and gather it to extinguish candles from a cake.

Most days, however, the ebb and flow of air in our chest, so vital for our cells to carry on their daily work, occurs without our input. God has designed us to breathe on automatic. He manages the business of our breathing, so we can focus on the work he's prepared for us to do (Eph. 2:10).

In the Hospital

Breathing demands our attention when it goes wrong. In such cases, the process that usually cycles in the background takes center stage. When we can't breathe, everything else is impossible too.

Perhaps you've experienced this horror during an asthma attack, when every breath ends in wheezing. Or maybe you've felt your chest tighten as doctors and nurses have scrambled to help you through an allergic reaction. If you've struggled with pneumonia, you know how the pain in your ribs sharpens with each breath, and the infection rattles beneath your breastbone. Maybe you've experienced the misery of fluid enveloping your lungs after a grueling illness. If you've dealt with fluid within the lungs themselves, you know how each breath, no matter how deep, never feels like enough. You strain even the muscles in your neck to breathe, but the satisfaction of that draft of air never comes.

Hospital measures offer welcome relief in such moments. You feel the cool stream of oxygen through cannula in your nostrils, and your tightly wound body relaxes, like a spring uncoiling. A mask covers your face, mist clouds your eyes, and your fists unclench. The panic subsides. You blink to clear away the tears, and then thank God for restoring your breathing.

Yet even these essential, life-saving gifts are measly substitutes for God's design. A ventilator transforms breathing from a gentle rhythm into a routine of force. It relies on positive pressure, meaning that rather than gently pulling air into your lungs, it *pushes* it. The machine pumps air according to a computer, and blares an alarm when the flow leaks out from your mask or when the pressure in your airways escalates too high. On a ventilator, our breathing transitions from the realm of the unconscious into the domain of electrical cords and digital consoles.

Even if we don't require a ventilator, a sudden reliance upon supplemental oxygen can stir up unease. The very air, blanketing and nourishing the entire earth, is no longer sufficient to sustain us. Where we once walked freely, we can now go only if we bring tanks with sufficient liters of oxygen. Tubing tethers us to the world of the unwell.

Before Heaven

As you glance at that tubing, or again strap on the mask, or fight against the anxiety that swells when your breathing tightens, one truth persists: you remain in God's grip.

God breathed life into you while you slept in your mother's womb. He drew it from you when as an infant you burst into the light. Even now, as you strive and pray, he fills your weary lungs with air.

When he proclaimed the gospel to the Athenians in the book of Acts, Paul remarked, "The God who made the world and everything in it, being Lord of heaven and earth, does not live in temples made by man, nor is he served by human hands, as though he needed anything, since he himself gives to mankind all life and *breath* and everything" (Acts 17:24–25). His words echo Isaiah, who affirms God as the Lord "who spread out the earth and what comes from it, / who gives *breath* to the people on it / and spirit to those who walk in it" (Isa. 42:5). Job also remembers from whom he musters breath: "In his hand is the life of every living thing and the *breath* of all mankind" (Job 12:10).

Sin warps our breathing, but it can't erase the truth that our very breath is a gift from God. He instilled you with breath so that as his image bearer, you might know him, enjoy him, and glorify him. When disease constricts your breathing, every gust of air remains a gift from him.

Eventually, our last breath will escape us and dissipate into the air. Our bodies will fade, and the work of our hands will blow away. Yet even though death transiently claims us, God's love for us has triumphed over death, and endures forever:

> As for man, his days are like grass;
> he flourishes like a flower of the field;

for the wind passes over it, and it is gone,
and its place knows it no more.
But the steadfast love of the LORD is from everlasting to
everlasting on those who fear him. (Ps. 103:15–17)

The Breath of Life

Where do we find assurance of this steadfast love? When our chest aches, and when the simple act of breathing feels like misery, how can we know that God still holds us in his palms? How can we believe this?

The answer lies at the foot of the cross.

When sin threatened to strangle us, God's Son took on human breath. He condescended to become as one of us, in the flesh. For us, he gave up life, breath, and everything: "And the curtain of the temple was torn in two. Then Jesus, calling out with a loud voice, said, 'Father, into your hands I commit my spirit!' And having said this he breathed his last" (Luke 23:45–46).

God so loves you that he gave his Son to endure the same gasps and pangs that afflict you. When your chest tightens, remember that Christ's did also. When oxygen tubing tethers you to a bed, *remember that he gave his last breath so you would have eternal life.* Remember that even now, the Holy Spirit, the Lord and giver of life, breathes new life into you, to beautify you for the new heavens and the new earth.

Remember that when your breathing finally ceases, this same Lord will instill the breath of life into you again, not for a lifetime, but for all eternity.

Heavenly Father, we owe every breath in our lungs, whether smooth or strained, to your grace. Help us to remember that even as we struggle for air, you breathe new life into us through the Holy Spirit and promise us eternal life through Christ. Help us to trust in you when our breathing quickens, and to savor each draft of air. To you be all the glory, in Jesus's name. Amen.

11

Great Is Your Faithfulness

The steadfast love of the LORD never ceases;
his mercies never come to an end;
they are new every morning;
great is your faithfulness.

LAMENTATIONS 3:22–23

TWO YEARS BEFORE his diseased lungs confined him to hospital beds and breathing machines, my friend David delivered a speech about gratitude to an audience of 350 people in Boston. He worried about the event for days beforehand. The hosting institution was secular, as were the majority of the audience, but David couldn't speak about gratitude without also sharing his testimony. David prayed no one would storm out.

The following is an excerpt of the speech he gave that day:

In 1986, I became homeless and addicted to drugs on the streets of New York City. I wandered New York for almost 10 years searching for the next high. At my rock-bottom I attempted suicide but I failed. During my attempt, grace was shown toward me by a total stranger who witnessed what I had tried to do. He very quietly approached me and started talking to me. He showed me undeserved grace. Undeserved because we did not know each other and he owed me nothing. But yet, there he was talking to me as if my life mattered to him.

Almost an hour and a half later, I found myself walking into Bellevue hospital where this stranger waited and watched while I was examined and then admitted into the hospital. He disappeared and I never saw him again. Many people would refer to him as a Good Samaritan. I referred to him as an angel. Because just like the angels in the Bible stories you may have heard, he had a message for me, which was that my life was worth living because I, like all of you, am a unique creation who was formed in God's own image, packed full of potential, who deserves to love, be loved, and live life to the fullest. . . .

I am grateful for the loving and compassionate God who gave me so much undeserved grace by sending a stranger to help me in time of desperate need.

I am grateful for the love and understanding my family gave me and the undeserved grace they showed me by opening their arms and welcoming me back into the fold. . . .

I am grateful that through the grace of God I have been clean and sober since 1998 and counting.

And last but never least, I am beyond grateful that all of you have allowed me to come here tonight and stand before you as a happy and productive member of society, to share with you my life and, in so doing, without realizing it, have shown me such undeserved grace.[1]

1 Reprinted from personal correspondence.

When David finished, he raised his eyes and was taken aback to see the moderator weeping. Slowly, members of the crowd rose to their feet. They gave him a standing ovation.

"I left humbled and secure in the knowledge that God will be praised no matter what my thoughts and misgivings are!" he wrote to me afterward.

Just two years later, David sat across from me in his hospital room with oxygen tubing snaking into his nostrils, and struggled with misgivings anew.

The Soul Bowed Down

Despair took hold of David insidiously, like an undertow drawing him away from solid ground. At first he attributed his worsening shortness of breath to smoke exposure, from roommates whom he suspected used cigarettes on the sly. A move to another apartment, however, didn't solve the problem. Then, doctors told him he had recurrent bouts of pneumonia, which antibiotics should fix. They didn't. His breathing became worse and worse, and soon he could no longer sing the hymns that so comforted him. Before long, an oxygen tank was his constant companion. He couldn't walk more than a few feet without having to pause and use a nebulizer.

On the worst days, when the constant ricocheting between hospital and rehab wore him down, his grasp of God's goodness also faded away. He'd harbored God's word in his heart for decades, but when delirium swamped his mind, he struggled to withdraw verses from the fog.

"I'm scared," he said that day, while my kids scribbled in coloring books. "I just don't understand what God is doing. I just keep praying over and over for him to forgive me."

"Do you believe Jesus died for you, David?" I'd asked him.

That question still hung in the air, looming in the background as the days rolled on.

For years, through all the adversity he faced, David had so clearly grasped God's love and provision. But as his days in the hospital tallied up, the grace of God, which had stirred his heart for so long and moved 350 people to their feet, seemed a distant memory. The miseries of tight lungs and cold hospital rooms were too much.

New Mercies Every Morning

And yet, great is God's faithfulness.

David's hope dwindled, but God's steadfast love for him didn't cease. He remembered David, just as he remembered Jeremiah weeping over the ruins of Jerusalem:

> Remember my affliction and my wanderings,
>   the wormwood and the gall!
> My soul continually remembers it
>   and is bowed down within me.
> But this I call to mind,
>   and therefore I have hope:
> The steadfast love of the LORD never ceases;
>   his mercies never come to an end;
> they are new every morning;
>   great is your faithfulness. (Lam. 3:19–23)

God's faithfulness sings out from every book of the Bible. "The LORD your God is God, the faithful God who keeps covenant and steadfast love with those who love him and keep his commandments, to a thousand generations," Moses declares in Deuteronomy 7:9. God remembered Noah when the floodwaters reached their zenith (Gen. 8:1). He sealed his covenant with Abraham by walking, *himself*, among the torn animal sacrifices, invoking a curse upon himself should he break his promise (Gen. 15:17). He saved a remnant of Israel to return to Jerusalem out of exile (Ezra 9:8), and through that remnant kept his promise to preserve the authority of David's line in Judah (Zech. 4:8–10). He remained faithful to his covenant people when they groaned beneath the oppression of slavery (Ex. 2:25).

When our soul bows down in grief, and we lie prostrate amid the rubble of our ruined lives, God remains faithful. His steadfast love never ceases. His mercies never come to an end.

A few weeks after our conversation, David called me. He was still in the hospital, and he'd been struggling with paranoia from high carbon dioxide levels, so I felt a twinge of anxiety when I saw his number. Would he be fearful and suspicious, or his loving, witty self? Could he perceive God's faithfulness, or had his ordeals chipped away at his faith permanently? *Please, Lord, help me to show him your face*, I prayed.

When I heard his voice, I sighed with relief. He was lucid again, and sounded like himself. He was also crying.

"Katie, I'm calling because I need to tell you something. You've been a light of grace to me. Scott and the kids too. I'm so thankful that God brought you all into my life." He paused. "I don't know how much longer I have, and I need to say this while I can."

I leaned forward with my head in my free hand. The relief, gratitude, and sorrow felt like a tide, admixing, flooding over. I started to cry myself, and searched for the right words to say. All I could manage was, "We love you, David."

"I'm doing okay, Katie. I've been in a dark place, but God's shown me how near he is." He paused again. "And I know that because of Jesus, I'm forgiven."

"Whatever happens, David, God loves you. You know that he loves you."

"I know. He's shown me. Do you remember Isaiah 6? When Isaiah sees God on his throne, and his robe fills the temple? This morning when I woke up, God showed me that scene. And I could *see it*—all his glory, his robe flowing down. Just the *hem* of his robe filled the room. God is so much bigger than any of this. And he's near. He's so close. Closer than any of us realizes." Coughing broke up his words, and when he regained himself he drew a tight breath. "I know where I'm headed now, Katie. I'm still scared of going through it, but I'm not scared of *where* I'm going anymore, because I know I'll be with him."

"And you'll be belting out 'Witness' before the heavenly hosts," I joked.

He laughed, and tried to answer, but another coughing fit prevented him. The laughter, and the words spoken, were enough.

The steadfast love of the Lord never ceases. His mercies never come to an end.

Great is his faithfulness.

The Train of His Robe Filled the Temple

God reassured David of his love through the account of Isaiah's commissioning:

In the year that King Uzziah died I saw the Lord sitting upon a throne, high and lifted up; and the train of his robe filled the temple. Above him stood the seraphim. Each had six wings: with two he covered his face, and with two he covered his feet, and with two he flew. And one called to another and said:

"Holy, holy, holy is the LORD of hosts;
The whole earth is full of his glory!" (Isa. 6:1–3)

In the next verses, we see that Isaiah's response to this magnificent display of God's glory wasn't solace, but rather *panic*. "And the foundations of the thresholds shook at the voice of him who called, and the house was filled with smoke," the passage continues. "And I said: 'Woe is me! For I am lost; for I am a man of unclean lips, and I dwell in the midst of a people of unclean lips; for my eyes have seen the King, the LORD of hosts!" (Isa. 6:4–5). Isaiah knew that before a holy God he had no power to stand. The glory that filled the temple shone a spotlight on Isaiah's every sin. Like Isaiah, before our holy God we cower, broken by our wrongdoings, wretched in depravity, because "there is none who does good, not even one" (Ps. 14:3; 53:3).

How could my friend David rejoice in this scene that drove Isaiah trembling to his knees? How could this passage possibly comfort him?

Because he had the full story.

David knew the ending. The image of God's robe billowing through the doorway reminded him that God's power covers even our worst afflictions. The power that shook the temple and frightened Isaiah to his bones also washed David clean through the blood of Christ. When Jesus died upon the cross, the temple curtain tore in two from top to bottom (Matt. 27:51), and my friend David knew that once he quit this earth, with that cloth ripped away he would bask in God's resplendence. When breath escaped his chest for the last time, he would approach God in all his glory, enter into the presence of holiness that not even seraphim could gaze upon, and relax into the Father's embrace as a beloved, adopted son (Rom. 8:15; Eph. 1:5).

Isaiah 6 reminded David that while he struggled to breathe, he remained in the grip of the one who first gave him breath. The one whom angels praised with "holy, holy, holy!" was sovereign even over the hallways and the monitors, the wheezing and the tubes. And that same God, whose robe filled the temple, had secured David a home in heaven through Christ.

Great is his faithfulness.

PART 3

BY GRACE YOU
HAVE BEEN SAVED

Remembering What God Has Done

*But God, being rich in mercy, because of the great love
with which he loved us, even when we were dead in our
trespasses, made us alive together with Christ—by grace
you have been saved—and raised us up with him and
seated us with him in the heavenly places in Christ Jesus,
so that in the coming ages he might show the immeasurable
riches of his grace in kindness toward us in Christ Jesus.*

EPHESIANS 2:4–7

12

Why Have You Forsaken Me?

My God, my God, why have you forsaken me?
Why are you so far from saving me, from the words of
my groaning?
O my God, I cry by day, but you do not answer,
and by night, but I find no rest.

PSALM 22:1–2

I GLANCED AT the cardiac monitor, and my heart sank as the interval between his heartbeats lengthened. Blood oozing within his fractured skull was crowding out his brain.

Paramedics had rushed him to the ER after someone bludgeoned him with a baseball bat in his sleep. His wife, who had been lying beside him, died during the assault. His four-year-old son witnessed everything.

As the neurosurgery team prepared an operating room, I raced to reduce the swelling with medications through a specialized catheter. I struggled to focus. The work required precision, but thoughts of the little boy distracted me. I envisioned him staggering down the hallway in footed pajamas, rubbing his eyes with a fist, then opening them to watch his world disintegrate with the crack of a bat. I considered the images that would forever emblazon his mind, the brutality no child should ever witness, that he now knew as intimately as his mother's embrace. *What kind of life was he going to have, with such memories haunting him?*

While I still wrestled with this thought, paramedics careened into the ER with a teenager dying from a gunshot wound. His heart had stopped, and they were performing chest compressions to force blood to his brain.

My junior resident took my place, and I rushed to help this new victim. A wise nurse had already opened a surgical kit, and in a blur I grasped a scalpel and explored the young boy's chest. I cupped his still heart, and searched its borders with trembling fingers. When my hand plunged into a gaping hole, I caught my breath. The bullet had torn open his aorta, which then emptied his blood volume into his chest.

We couldn't save him.

Silence overtook the room, and I backpedaled from the stretcher in a daze. My eyes flitted from his face, to the wound I'd created in futility, and back again. He was just a kid. His eyes peered from beneath half-closed lids, and blood streaked his neck, but the curves of his face still hinted at the promise and adventure of youth. My eyes fell to my own arms, stained to the elbows with blood. I had cradled his innermost parts, yet I'd never heard his laugh or the tenor of his voice. Now, thanks to the work of a violent hand and the failures of my own, no one would ever again.

I wanted to retreat to a call room, to cry and process the tragedy, but our work wasn't done. We still needed to inform his family.

After changing my scrubs, I found his aunt and uncle leaning against one another in the waiting room, their arms intertwined like branches. During the long walk to a private room, they never let go of each other. The knuckles of their clasped hands whitened as I retold the horrible events.

"We brought him here for a better life," his aunt wailed. "His mother is back in Guatemala. How do I tell her?"

Words felt too thick in my throat to give an answer. What solace could I possibly offer her? What answers could I give to soften the cruelty of this loss? I could discern none, and so said nothing.

Everything was wrong.

My trauma pager blared yet again. Another teenaged kid. Another gunshot wound. This time, the bullet had struck the boy's head.

The room didn't resound this time, because inevitable death has a way of muting things. Movements slow. Voices drop a few decibels, partly in reverence, partly in defeat. The resident, perceiving the situation the moment the patient entered the room, conducted his exam in a murmur.

Paramedics had intubated the boy and ventilated him with oxygen, so his heart still beat, but he wasn't breathing on his own. When the resident shined a light into his eyes, his pupils remained fixed, empty, staring into the unseen. We all recognized the signs. Brain death had claimed him, and we had no help to offer.

Mustering my dwindling reserves, I began to suture his head wound closed. The least I could do, I thought, was to mend his wound and to clean him, to give his family a final, familiar glimpse of the boy they loved.

Midway through my work, the door opened. I raised my eyes, then froze in dread as his mother walked into the room.

Blood still haloed her son's head. Fragments of his brain clung to my gloves. As her face contorted, I knew she took it all in, every detail, every gash and fleck of this horrible scene etched into her memory forever.

She howled, and fell to the floor.

I tugged the bloodied gloves from my hands, rushed from the room, and hid my face as I sobbed.

Searching for God

The next morning I wandered about as if lost. I'd dealt with tragedy in the ER before, but not like this. The victims were all so young, the attacks all so ruthless. In each case, someone had looked at a young man and saw *no worth*. For these assailants to so recklessly take life meant they didn't value it at all. How could their hearts be so deadened? How could God allow such evil?

For decades, my meager faith had reposed untested within my heart. I grew up as a nominal Christian in a family that upheld Christian traditions with a heavily secular slant. Santa Claus, rather than Jesus, assumed center stage at Christmas. We never discussed the gospel. We never read the Bible or went to church. I prayed, but had no idea to whom. I understood Christianity as synonymous with good behavior and sentimentality.

With no backbone to support it, my faith came crashing down that morning in the ER. I'd been working on my feet for over twenty-four hours, but when my shift ended, instead of heading home to sleep I drove one hundred miles into the Berkshire Mountains. I wove for hours along tree-rimmed vistas and watched the autumn foliage scroll past the windshield in fiery mosaics. For the duration of the drive, I tried to reconcile the evil I'd witnessed. *How could God allow such suffering?* I lamented. *How could such a God be good? How could a just God exist and yet tolerate such evil?*

I stopped at a bridge spanning the Connecticut River, which unspooled in a vein of quicksilver toward the horizon. On either side of the river, hills swathed in gold and scarlet heaped upward to stand guard against a clear sky. I grasped the railing and felt the wind stir my hair. Surely, I could connect with God here. I parted my lips to pray.

No words came.

I yearned for him, but all I could see was blood. Vacant, lifeless eyes. The agonized expressions of the mother, the aunt and uncle. Only a few thoughts broke through: *How could these families endure? Where was God in all this? Why didn't he intervene? How could he allow evil to taint the world he'd created?*

A gust of wind and the crescendo of a passing car spoke into my ears. I strained to hear God's reply. After a lifetime of living apart from his word, I didn't know how else to listen for his voice.

No answer came.

Even if I had acknowledged God's love imprinted in the light that danced between river and sky, without Scripture my faith was left dry. In the vast silence, with no understanding of God's word, I decided I couldn't discern an answer because he didn't exist.

Thereafter, I plunged into the worst depressive episode of my life. Without God infusing the world with purpose, life held little meaning. Despair tarnished everything. Beauty dulled. Joy drained away as if down a sinkhole.

In this ghostly state, existing but not thriving, I ruminated daily over taking my own life. Every night as the lights of Boston receded behind me, I fought the impulse to drive to that bridge over the Connecticut River and hurl myself over the railing. Only love for my husband, whose heart I couldn't break, kept me from the icy water.[1]

My God, Why Have You Forsaken Me?

Dark seasons can swallow us up. When disaster strikes or grief engulfs us, we wander through a wasteland in search of God. We cry out to him, but hear only the echo of our own voice. We search our hearts and minds for his truth, but find the terrain windswept, the words blown away.

Against this landscape, a familiar refrain captures our heartache: "My God, my God, why have you forsaken me?" (Ps. 22:1).

Scripture first attributes these words to David, a man after God's own heart (1 Sam. 13:14). David wasn't morally superior to his contemporaries, and in fact he committed some awful acts (2 Sam. 11:3–4, 14–15), but he *trusted* in God. As a boy he dared to challenge the behemoth warrior Goliath, whom no soldier could defeat, because he had faith in God's provision: "The LORD who delivered me from the paw of the lion and from the paw of the bear will deliver me from the hands of this Philistine" (1 Sam. 17:37). He inquired first of the Lord before making any major decisions (1 Sam. 23:1–5), and wrote praise songs that would extoll God's steadfast love for centuries to come (Ps. 145).

Yet even David, God's chosen king and faithful servant, endured dark nights of the soul. "Why are you so far from saving me, from the words of my groaning?" he laments in Psalm 22. "O my God,

1 Adapted from my article "A Critical Care Surgeon Meets the Great Physician," *Christianity Today*, February 17, 2017, https://www.christianitytoday.com/ct/2017/march/critical-care -surgeon-meets-great-physician.html.

I cry by day, but you do not answer, and by night, but I find no rest" (Ps. 22:1–2). His words remind us that as we toil in a sin-stricken world, even those who love God spend seasons wandering through the wilderness. In David's case, suffering so penetrated his soul that only poetry could mine its depths: "I am poured out like water, / and all my bones are out of joint; / my heart is like wax; / it is melted within my breast; / my strength is dried up like a potsherd, / and my tongue sticks to my jaws; / you lay me in the dust of death" (Ps. 22:14–15).

Even David flailed in the darkness. As sorrow seizes us, our shared struggle with him in Psalm 22 can offer a cool cup of water for our parched souls.

And when we consider who also referenced Psalm 22, that well opens up. The foundations crack. A tide breaks through, pouring forth oceans.

A Man of Sorrows

David composed Psalm 22 in a flight of God-breathed inspiration, but Jesus then quoted it from the cross. Matthew 27:46 tells us the following: "And about the ninth hour Jesus cried out with a loud voice, saying, 'Eli, Eli, lema sabachthani?' that is, 'My God, my God, why have you forsaken me?'"

Pause and consider this carefully. God's own Son, who loved the Father before the world began (John 17:24), felt cut off from God on the cross. The Son, whom the Father called beloved (Matt. 3:17; 17:5), who was "the radiance of the glory of God and the exact imprint of his nature" (Heb. 1:3), who for all eternity had been in loving communion with the Father (John 8:58), cried out to that same Father with desperate longing. He searched the heavens for God, and found them empty.

This is astonishing. The nails tearing through nerve and sinew, the wounds weeping on Jesus's back, and the gasps to breathe were torture enough. Yet while suspended on that terrible tree, Jesus also descended into the deepest valleys of spiritual suffering. The weight of our sins not only broke him in body, but also sent the cosmic penalty we deserve barreling down upon him: separation from God. Banishment from the one with whom he shared eternity. Exile from him whom he adoringly called, "Abba, Father" (Mark 14:36).

Scripture promises us that "we do not have a high priest who is unable to sympathize with our weaknesses, but one who in every respect has been tempted as we are, yet without sin" (Heb. 4:15). Our Savior was "a man of sorrows and acquainted with grief" (Isa. 53:3). Like us, he wept in the face of loss (John 11:35). In the quiet of Gethsemane, trembling before the oncoming wrath, he said, "My soul is very sorrowful, even to death" (Mark 14:34).

When we despair in the dark of a hospital room, or hover in the silent wake of a life vanished, or search for God on a windswept bridge, we can reap solace from Christ. When our eyes fail to discern evidence of God's love, we can cling to the truth that *he knows our suffering*, because he endured it too. And stunningly, he bore it *for us*. He took on the full weight of our sin and absorbed the punishment we earned, purely out of loving obedience to the Father, who in turn so loved us (John 3:16).

Yet God's story of redemption through Christ doesn't begin and end with suffering. Even in his plaintive cry to the Father, Jesus points to our everlasting hope.

He Has Done It

Psalm 22 is a messianic psalm. When Jesus quotes verse 2, he not only yearns for the Father, but *he also declares that the psalm is about him.* Jesus identifies himself as the one "scorned by mankind and despised by the people" (Ps. 22:6). The verse, "He trusts in the LORD; let him deliver him; let him rescue him, for he delights in him!" (Ps. 22:8) foretold the insults the elders and scribes hurled at Jesus: "He trusts in God; let God deliver him now, if he desires him" (Matt. 27:43). Jesus's bones were stretched out of joint (Ps. 22:14). His hands and feet were pierced (Ps. 22:16). His were the clothes, lying limp upon the ground, that the soldiers divided and then bartered by lots (Ps. 22:18; John 19:24).

At the conclusion of Psalm 22, after weaving such a heartrending picture of suffering, David finds hope *in Jesus.* He didn't yet know Jesus's name, or face, or the year he would humble himself to lie in a manger, but at the close of Psalm 22 David rejoices in God's promised Messiah. A thousand years before Mary traveled to Bethlehem, the promise of her Son was the ray of light that pierced through David's despair:

> All the prosperous of the earth eat and worship;
>> before him shall bow all who go down to the dust,
>> even the one who could not keep himself alive.
> Posterity shall serve him;
>> it shall be told of the Lord to the coming generation;
> they shall come and proclaim his righteousness to a people yet
>> unborn,
>> that he has done it. (Ps. 22:29–31)

When he wallowed in affliction, King David clung to hope in Christ. A wellspring of hope now issues forth from the bloody cross, because through his agony, Jesus declares, *I am he. I am the one whose coming was foretold* (Matt. 11:2–6). *I am the one who was mocked, who is now making all things new* (Rev. 21:5). *I am the one, as even now your sins crush you, who will wipe away every tear* (Rev. 21:4).

I didn't know Christ the day I stood on that bridge and searched for God. I didn't know the promise celebrated in the Psalms, the hope that buoyed the patriarchs through famine and persecution. Yet while I agonized and gripped the railing, God had already brought that hope to glorious fruition.

In Christ, he has done it.

13

By His Wounds

He himself bore our sins in his body on the tree,
that we might die to sin and live to righteousness.
By his wounds you have been healed.

1 PETER 2:24

MY KIDS ROUTINELY demand Band-Aids for paper cuts.

We've all felt the quick sting of these slivers while flipping through pages of a book. They hurt for a few seconds, rarely bleed, and always heal without a trace in a day or two. Yet without fail, after the flash of pain shocks them from their construction paper endeavors, my kids run to me with a finger held aloft, eyes welling, and plead for a bandage.

"This doesn't need a Band-Aid, honey," I used to say, after a hug and a kiss. "It will heal just fine."

I don't say that anymore.

I'm both a doctor and their mom. But my reassurances mean bupkes against what they see: the skin sliced open, a pink trace of tissue visible. "It looks like it might bleed!" they'd always retort. "I can see a bit of red!"

I've learned to just give them the Band-Aid.

Wounds of the Flesh

Our aversion to wounds is instinctive. The sight of blood claims the equilibrium of even the most rugged of men (which I learned the hard way in medical school, when I foolishly tried to suture a gentleman's hand wound without insisting that he lie down first). Wounds unveil what's meant to be hidden, displaying a backwardness we'd prefer not to confront. A paper cut betrays only a hint of pink, and yet even a child knows this breach in the skin is wrong, and hastens to conceal it.

We can dismiss paper cuts, but the perverseness is more obvious with open wounds that expose our anatomy to the world. A yellow marbling of fat poking from beneath the skin or a strap of muscle lurking in a wound bed signals a reversal of God's intended order. We can push through pain and muster courage to endure stitches, but the sight of blood and tendon open to the air sickens us, as if we've been turned inside out.

Even the pristine, controlled incision from a surgery leaves a memorandum that something has gone wrong. Whether an operation gives you a pale wisp of scar or a twisted rope of flesh snaking down your torso, the marks we bear remind us that doctors needed to enter spaces previously off-limits. While we heal, we'll never forget that we needed something excised, or repaired, or reconfigured, because something within us wasn't right.

When Wounds Heal

In the simplest cases, wounds afflict us for a short time, and then they heal over. A few days with a Band-Aid, and the skin seals.

Others wounds are far more complicated.

If you've dealt with an infected surgical incision that required reopening, or a ragged, gaping wound too contaminated to close, you know the long, tedious course that follows. Clinicians perform "wet-to-dry" dressings several times daily, peeling off an adherent layer of gauze to abrade slough from the wound bed. Sometimes during these dressing changes, a surgical resident will whittle away dead tissue with a scissor or scalpel before repacking the wound. In eight hours, a different clinician repeats the routine, over and over, day in and day out.

Even this tedious process doesn't compare with the challenges posed by wounds recalcitrant to healing, the ones that persist and suppurate despite our very best medical techniques. Ischemic foot ulcers are an example. Those whose arteries calcify over time can develop leg pain with walking or sleeping, and then discover one morning that a wound has opened on a foot. Such wounds, sometimes barely the size of a dime, are more ominous than the most grotesque gash because they signal a threatened limb. Without blood flow, the crater can't heal, and over time infection tunnels to bone. Unless surgeons reroute blood vessels to deliver a fresh supply to the foot, amputation is inevitable.

While ischemic ulcers are foreboding, fistulas are a nightmare to manage. They arise when infection or trauma within the abdomen tears a rent in the intestines, and the spilled contents, rich in enzymes that degrade fat and protein, erode through the abdominal wall. The result is an inflamed tunnel between the intestines and the outside world that gushes caustic fluid. As fistula drainage leaks, it thieves away critical nutrients, depletes electrolytes, and corrodes the skin raw. One young man who developed multiple fistulas after a gunshot wound to the abdomen required placement of a complex dressing, including tubes and a giant sponge connected to a vacuum device, three times a week, in the operating room, under general anesthesia, for a *year*. When he finally left the hospital, by

God's grace he was alive, but the fistula had left him emaciated, jaundiced, and unable to walk, a shadow of his former self. And he was barely twenty.

Then there are burns. While blades and bullets rip open and intestinal fluid eats away, heat destroys. The wounds that hurt most, ironically, are the easiest to manage: first degree burns pose no greater threat than a sunburn, and superficial second degree burns sting, but need only good wound care with an ointment.

More severe burns, by contrast, dive so deeply that they demolish nerves in their path. These wounds leave us numb, because the very mechanisms that alert us to pain are scorched away. Yet while we don't feel them, these burns are the most sinister because they expose our inner workings to the air. Without the protection of our skin, the water we need to support every bodily function evaporates. Our blood pressure plummets, and our organs, oxygen-starved, shut down.

In some cases, the wounds we can't feel are the most dangerous of all.

Your Wound Is Grievous

Sin guts all mankind with a sharpened blade. We witness its handiwork all around us: warfare, corruption, poverty, famine, abuse, violence, typhoons, oppression, earthquakes, pestilence. We bear its marks ourselves, the injustices and pain we suffer contorting us, the idolatry we commit ourselves blackening and desiccating all that's good. Our sins fester. Like fistulas, they ooze vitriol long after the sting of our wrongdoings abates. Like severe burns, they tunnel deep and clandestine, numbing us while they destroy what matters.

Whether through fire or corrosion, all sin earns us God's wrath, spoils our relationship with him, and places us squarely—and rightly—under his judgment.

In the book of Jeremiah we glimpse our dilemma. After the kingdom of Judah indulged in idolatrous practices for generations, repeatedly scoffing at God's mercy and discounting opportunities for repentance, God recruited Nebuchadnezzar as his instrument of judgment. The Babylonians besieged Jerusalem, destroyed the temple, and murdered multitudes. In the wake of the horror, God declared the following:

> For thus says the LORD:
> Your hurt is incurable,
> and your wound is grievous.
> There is none to uphold your cause,
> no medicine for your wound,
> no healing for you.
> All your lovers have forgotten you;
> they care nothing for you;
> for I have dealt you the blow of an enemy,
> the punishment of a merciless foe,
> because your guilt is great,
> because your sins are flagrant. (Jer. 30:12–14)

Judah's suffering is incurable because her sins are incurable. Like an ischemic ulcer eroding into bone, her sins burrow to the depths, corrupting everything.

As do ours. Just like the Jews in exile, we are lost in our sin, our hurt incurable, our wound grievous. As Paul says in his letter to the Romans, "All have turned aside; together they have become worthless; / no one does good, / not even one" (Rom. 3:12).

How many times have you fought to do the right thing, to conquer the desires that drag you away from God, only to wallow in lusts once more? "For I do not do the good I want," Paul says about this pattern, "but the evil I do not want is what I keep on doing" (Rom. 7:19). Isaiah describes us as sheep that have gone astray; "We have turned—every one—to his own way" (Isa. 53:6).

Without God's grace, the damage our sins inflict can never heal. The flesh cannot seal. The fibers will not hold. While we strive for remedies, and seek worldly tinctures to heal ourselves, the wounds only spread, splaying ever wider.

By His Wounds We Are Healed

But God, being rich in mercy, because of the great love with which he loves us (Eph. 2:4), will not let your wounds fester.

As the psalmist writes, God "heals the brokenhearted and binds up their wounds" (Ps. 147:3). Even in Jeremiah 30, after the Lord diagnosed Judah's wounds as incurable, he promised to heal them: "For I will restore health to you, / and your wounds I will heal, / declares the LORD, / because they have called you an outcast: / . . . And you shall be my people, / and I will be your God" (Jer. 30:17, 22). God pledged to restore Judah and Israel to the land he promised them centuries before, when Abraham looked to the stars (Gen. 15:5). No earthly medicines could soothe the hearts of the exiles in Babylon, but God would pour out his healing grace upon them, because God, as we've seen, is merciful, faithful, and abounding in steadfast love (Ex. 34:6).

God's promise to Judah was fulfilled seventy years later, when King Cyrus of Persia released the exiles to Jerusalem to rebuild the temple (Ezra 1:1–4). Yet Jeremiah's prophesy foretold an even grander, deeper, more magnificent restoration. In chapter 31, the Lord promises to forge a new covenant with his people:

Behold, the days are coming, declares the LORD, when I will make a new covenant with the house of Israel and the house of Judah, not like the covenant that I made with their fathers. . . . I will put my law within them, and I will write it on their hearts. And I will be their God, and they shall be my people. And no longer shall each one teach his neighbor and each his brother, saying, "Know the LORD," for they shall all know me, from the least of them to the greatest, declares the LORD. For I will forgive their iniquity, and I will remember their sin no more. (Jer. 31:31–34)

In these verses, Jeremiah prophesied the coming of the Messiah, the Christ, who once and for all would secure forgiveness for mankind, and heal our wounds forever. Even as our souls groan under the weight of our sins, and even as our wounds, still open, weep and throb, this side of the cross we can rejoice. Whatever slings and arrows this life hurls at us, and however we fail, Christ has redeemed us to God. Our sins were flagrant and our hurt incurable, but he has restored us such that through him, we are now without blemish. Our sores are mended. Our souls are without pockmark, scar, or gash. We are born again to a living hope, made new (1 Pet. 1:3). By Christ's stripes, we are healed (Isa. 53:5).

The wounds of our flesh leave scars. The wounds of our soul gnaw us from within. *But Christ's wounds heal everything.* His arms punctured through, the flesh of his back raw against the crossbeam, the laceration in his side that poured out water and blood—he bore all these for *our sake.* Their horror echoed the unseen, cataclysmic, supernatural wound Christ bore for us on the cross: the wrath of God we unleashed with our own hands, poured out on his beloved Son in our place.

Wet gauze, wrappings, and ointments can coax your fleshly wounds to close. But only Christ can heal your soul. And thanks be to God, because of the great love with which he loved us, Christ has already "borne our griefs and carried our sorrows" (Isa. 53:4). What our own meager hands could not accomplish, his wounds have already achieved.

While our injuries remind us of death, his wounds overcame death itself. And by his wounds, we are healed.

Heavenly Father, sin wounds us body and soul, leaving scars that never fade. We rejoice that when we were without a cure and without a hope, you sent your Son to bear our afflictions for us. By his wounds, we are healed. We laud your name and praise you! To you be all the honor and glory, forever and ever. Amen.

14

Wait for the Lord

Wait for the LORD;
  be strong, and let your heart take courage;
  wait for the LORD!

PSALM 27:14

"OH PLEASE, no more!"

My chief resident waited until the patient had wiped the tears from her face, then tried again. "I understand this isn't what you wanted to hear . . ."

"Oh stop it!" she cried. "Don't patronize me! You said I could go home, and now you're saying I can't. You're a liar!"

"I'm sorry for this. We did promise that you could go home. It's what you deserve."

"Then let me go!"

"I wish we could, but we can't. The scan showed another fluid collection."

"Why does this keep happening?" she said, glaring at him. "You're supposed to be the experts. Why can't you solve this problem?"

"The connection between your pancreas and intestines keeps leaking. It's a problem that's really hard to fix."

"But you people *made* that connection. You guys messed up, and I have to suffer for it. I should never have come here!"

"Nothing about this is right or okay." He studied her, and spoke the next words carefully. "But really . . . what is the alternative?"

She dropped her gaze, and fiddled with the bag, green with bile, that peaked from beneath her gown. She'd been in the hospital for three months, had seen few visitors, and had been away from home for so long that she couldn't recall the state of her kitchen table. For almost a hundred days, she'd waited for tests, scans, and pain medication in the dead of night, with no inkling of resolution. One day ago, we'd assured her that her long, arduous course was finally ending, and she could go home. Then, without warning, we'd rescinded our promise.

Who could blame her for her outburst?

"Sometimes I think dying of cancer would be better than this," she muttered. The indignation in her eyes had drained away, and sorrow brimmed over in its place. She dropped her head into her hands. "I'm just so tired of waiting."

Waiting Rooms

In every room of every hospital, people flit away hours of imposed idleness. Some of us wallow on stretchers until the CT scanner is free. Others glare at the clock, watching the hands complete yet another revolution without a long overdue conversation with a doctor. Those of us who've undergone surgery know the embarrassing wait for bowel function to resume, or for the physical therapist to clear us to go home.

In the best circumstances, waiting inflicts only minor annoyance. At other times, however, it grinds us down. If you've dealt with an unsettling diagnosis, you've spent nights untangling worries: *Will I need chemotherapy? Or surgery? What will this mean for my life? Who will care for my family? Will I be able to work? What will I do?* Day after day you wrestle with questions, with your only hope of answers an appointment weeks away.

We wait with clasped hands to hear critical news about those we love. *Will he wean from the ventilator, or awaken from the coma? Will he survive? Will I, if he doesn't recover?* While we await answers with our heads bowed in prayer, minutes can feel like decades.

We wait to go home and return to a normal life. We wait for a transplant. For a cure. For good news. For answers. For healing. For the pain to end.

While pain and grief can split us in two, the impact of waiting is more furtive. It chips away at our hope like a relentless sea eroding away the shore. Over time, our outlook, our strength, and even our faith yield and warp beneath the pummeling. As the days of our waiting lengthen, we wonder why God delays. We pine for his voice. "My soul waits for the Lord / more than the watchmen for the morning, / more than the watchmen for the morning," we read in Psalm 130:6, and we picture ourselves standing on a rampart, our eyes bleary with exhaustion, searching the horizon for relief. We scan the sky for God, and ache for his saving presence, because to our depths we all know that he alone is our Redeemer, our rock.

Still, the clock hands turn their monotonous pirouettes. The minutes bloat into hours without answers. We pray and we yearn, and still we wait.

A Legacy of Waiting

Trials of waiting obviously don't limit themselves to hospital corridors. Ever since Adam reached for the fatal fruit, all creation has waited with eager longing for God to make things right (Rom. 8:19). The Bible reveals that God's people have endured seasons of waiting for millennia.

The book of Exodus tells us the Egyptians "ruthlessly made the people of Israel work as slaves and made their lives bitter with hard service, in mortar and brick, and in all kinds of work in the field" (Ex. 1:13–14). Under the command of Pharaoh, Egyptian soldiers tore baby boys from their mothers and drowned them in the Nile (Ex. 1:15–16). This abuse persisted for *generations*. How earnestly the people must have cried out for relief!

In his faithfulness, God remembered his people, and liberated them with plagues, fire, and parted seas. Yet when they had finally tasted freedom, the Israelites worshiped the work of their own hands rather than God. As punishment, for forty years they wandered in the wilderness. They once again endured a long season of waiting, this time for redemption from an exile in the dust.

Centuries later, after the Babylonian siege, the Israelites waited seventy years to come home to Jerusalem. After their return, *four hundred years* of silence ensued. No prophets proclaimed. No new assurances stirred their hopes. For four centuries Israel held its breath, moaned beneath the oppression of successive conquerors, and awaited the fulfillment of God's promise from ages past: the coming of the Messiah, born in Bethlehem (Mic. 5:2), whom God would send to "bind up the brokenhearted, to proclaim liberty to the captives" (Isa. 61:1).

So many centuries later, we share in their longing. We wait not in arid wastelands or amid crumbled stones, but rather on operating tables, on stretchers, and in the strange, sterile rooms that house our worries.

They waited for Jesus to come. We wait for him to return.

Waiting for Our Blessed Hope

Even while we pray away the hours, this side of the cross God offers us a well from which even the patriarchs couldn't drink. While God's people in the Old Testament waited for salvation promised, we revel in salvation *fulfilled.* They hoped for the Messiah, but we *know him.* Through the Gospels, we can linger over the details of his miraculous work. We see him hung upon that bloody tree, the sky smoldering in his wake, and then we see him raised again, walking among those he loved, tasting the fish, rising to heaven to stir the host in glory.

When we stare into the night and urge the clock hands to speed their orbits, we can draw hope from the truth that our present anxieties, however they agitate us, are fleeting vapors. Paul reminds us that "this light momentary affliction is preparing for us an eternal weight of glory beyond all comparison, as we look not to the things that are seen but to the things that are unseen. For the things that are seen are transient, but the things that are unseen are eternal" (2 Cor. 4:17–18). The eternal unseen for which we wait is nothing less than *the everlasting presence of our loving God,* secured for us by one who walked through Jerusalem two thousand years ago. As we wring our hands, or press the call button again, or count the days until we can finally return home, as children of God (John 1:12) we are also "waiting for our blessed hope, the appearing of the glory of our great God and Savior Jesus Christ, who gave himself for us to redeem us from all lawlessness" (Titus 2:13–14).

For now, we wait. Hours and days lengthen. Time plods on. But against the promise of our blessed hope, these moments are ephemeral, a wisp of smoke that will disappear.

When Christ returns, every crack within our weary hearts will seal. Our aching bodies, and all their haywire malfunctions, will be made new (1 Cor. 15:49; Rev. 21:4). We will dwell forever with God, whose love gives rise to everything good (Mark 10:18).

Seasons of waiting grind us down. The slow passage of time taunts us. But Christ is coming. And when he returns, he will renew time itself.

15

God Shows His Love for Us

But God shows his love for us in that while we
were still sinners, Christ died for us.

ROMANS 5:8

FOR A YEAR, living felt an awful lot like dying.

After I walked away from God, I had no claim to hope. Nothing could anchor me through the hardships I routinely witnessed in the hospital. I discerned no meaning, no glint of mercy lining the dark moments. I saw only the horror of it all, the pervasive suffering. I saw how sin ruined everything. And I despaired.

During this season in the wilderness, I met Ron.[1] He was a bear of a man who loved spaghetti, especially on overloaded plates that reminded him of his Italian mother's generosity. He bellowed when he laughed. He also memorized the lyrics to cheesy eighties music, a talent incongruous with his heft and presence.

---

1   I wrote about Ron (a pseudonym) in "A Critical Care Surgeon Meets the Great Physician," *Christianity Today*, February 17, 2017, https://www.christianitytoday.com/ct/2017/march/critical-care-surgeon-meets-great-physician.html.

I didn't observe Ron's personality firsthand, but rather learned about him through stories his wife and grown children told as they stood vigil beside him day after day. In the middle of the night after undergoing a procedure, he'd suffered a cardiac arrest. His pulse returned after twenty minutes of CPR, but his long period without oxygen inflicted severe brain damage. When I met him weeks later, Ron would open his eyes, but show no awareness of his surroundings. Neurologists predicted he might eventually track objects with his eyes, but otherwise he would never meaningfully interact. While his heart still beat and his lungs breathed, his booming laughter seemed gone forever.

Ron's family hovered at his bedside and prayed for a miracle, and whenever I stopped by to examine him, they would prompt me for words of hope. I hated that I had none to give them. When I felt their eyes upon me, my cheeks would flush. I wanted to offer comfort, but I had no confidence that the boisterous, football-loving, belly-laughing man they adored would ever acknowledge them again.

Your Faith Has Healed You

One morning, a sudden chorus of eighties pop songs disrupted the ICU. Following the voice, I found Ron's wife at his bedside. She wore a cross the size of an avocado around her neck, and another dangled above Ron's head. She was cradling his hand beneath her chin, and singing as no Debbie Gibson fan ever had before. When she saw me step in, she beamed.

"Hi, Dr. Butler!"

"Is everything okay?"

"Oh, yes! I was praying and praying last night, and when I woke up, I knew everything would be fine. God told me Ron's going to be just fine."

My heart sank. I admired her conviction and her optimism, especially as I had neither. Yet her husband's clinical data suggested that everything would *not* be fine. Plus, I was convinced the God upon whom she leaned was a figment of her imagination.

"I hope that's the case," I said, trying to mask my doubt.

For the next week, every day she clung to Ron and crooned songs he loved. She prayed aloud and shouted blessings to everyone who passed her in the unit.

My colleagues and I tried to conceal our worry. How long before this blind hope fizzled? Upon what would she lean when it dissolved? We would shake our heads, and cast each other glances that said, *This is heartbreaking.*

One afternoon she shouted for me, and I trudged into the room, dreading the conversation. She'd already been through so much, and I didn't want to add to her hurt with the cold, merciless truth.

"Dr. Butler!" she cried when I entered. "He moved his toe when we asked!"

This is so sad, I thought. *How can I be gentle about this?* "This happens a lot in brain injuries," I said carefully. "It can be really confusing to see, but sometimes the spinal cord still triggers reflex movements, even when the brain –"

"No," she insisted. "That's not what this was. This was real. He *moved*. He heard me."

My stomach twisted. To humor her, I leaned within inches of Ron's ear. "Ron! Move your right toe!" I shouted.

Nothing.

"I'm sorry. It was probably just a reflex."

"No. It wasn't," she insisted. "*Watch.*" She put a hand on his shoulder, and shouted the same command into his ear.

He moved his toe.

She looked at me in triumph. I wanted to rejoice with her, but his MRI scans, the brain tissue darkened with dead neurons, overwhelmed the glimmer of progress before us. "I hope it means something," was all I could mutter. Inwardly, I believed it didn't.

The next day, he turned his head toward her. This was harder to ignore, but I was still unconvinced.

Then, he blinked to command.

In a week, he was awake.

In two weeks, he sat in a chair.

Days later, he motioned to his feeding tube, and mouthed the words, "Filet mignon?" Then he laughed, his tracheostomy blasting a guffaw of air.

At best, our neurologists had anticipated Ron might occasionally track moving objects. No one expected him to completely recover, as if no injury had ever afflicted him.

How could we explain his stunning improvement? How could we rationalize the sudden rewiring of neurons, winding the damage back like the hands of a clock?

Medical science offered no neat answers. No algorithm, statistical model, or chemical compound could repair brain injury like this. No textbook offered such brilliant methods for restoring a beloved father and husband to his family. Our gloved hands, skilled but finite, couldn't procure such healing.

We called his case an "outlier." We figured it was one of those rare situations that cheats statistics, that laughs in the face of graphs and projections.

But I remembered the cross suspended above his bed. His wife had prayed with such conviction. In the wake of that prayer, in the face of a hundred data points depicting zero hope, his distinctive laugh had resurfaced.

Through this outlier, a greater power had made himself known.

The Lord Is Patient toward You

Ron wandered through the valley of the shadow of death. In my unbelief and despair, so did I. Yet God broke through the darkness, and with one glorious expression of mercy, he ushered us both back into his light.

My transformation within that light wasn't instantaneous. Although I couldn't dismiss the power I'd witnessed at Ron's bedside, the memories that had haunted me for over a year still stirred up questions. *Perhaps God does exist,* I acceded. *But in the face of suffering, can we say he's good?*

I'm ashamed to admit that despite the prayers Ron's wife recited in Jesus's name, I first sought answers elsewhere. I presumed my cultural familiarity with Christianity meant I already "knew" it. In a brash display of arrogance, instead of the Bible, I searched the Bhagavad Gita, the Koran, the sprawling philosophies of Hinduism, and the eightfold path of Buddhism (an atheistic religion!) for the God who'd revealed himself to me in the ICU.

Of course, I found him in none of these traditions. There were points of wisdom and some poignant reflections, but coursing throughout all the texts was an assertion that somehow, by meditation or submission or good works, we could achieve our own righteousness.

I'd seen enough in the trauma bay to know that if our salvation depended on our own efforts, mankind was doomed. There was an element of chaos in the world that I didn't understand at the time, but saw daily. During my long shifts into the night, I'd watch illness and accidents claim the lives of scores of people who'd devoted their time and talents to improving the world.

They labored, sweated, strived, and sacrificed, clinging to dreams of charity and progress, yet all arrived through the same sliding doors on stretchers, with zero control over whether they lived or died. Their personal efforts to live upright lives couldn't halt the bus careening toward them or steady them against tumbling off the balcony.

Even a cursory survey of history revealed that a perverse chaos seemed to unravel the efforts of humanity. The steam engine revolutionized our abilities to produce and travel, but so increased demand for coal that thousands of miners died from accidents, suffocation, and black lung. After the invention of the cotton gin, production in America skyrocketed, but so too did the abomination of slavery. A rule of life, it seemed, was that horrible consequences would writhe up from our good intentions.

That rule, of course, was sin. I didn't know its name, because I didn't know Christ. But I'd seen enough of its malice to know we couldn't conquer it on our own. It had embedded itself into too many human hearts, and burned the hands of too many who railed against it. I knew we needed a Savior.

God, long-suffering, patient, and merciful with me after I denied him for so long (2 Pet. 3:9), was preparing my heart and mind to understand who that Savior was.

God Shows His Love for Us

For over a year during my struggle with depression, I resisted my husband Scott's urgings to join him at church. On the rare occasions when I acquiesced and attended, I was stalwart in my unbelief. While fellow congregants recited the word, prayed, and lifted up hymns, I would sit with my arms barred across my chest, my gaze defiant, my thoughts entrenched in skepticism.

Still, Scott urged me to read Scripture. My reply was consistently no—until I witnessed Ron's recovery in the ICU. Thanks be to God, the Spirit worked through that blessing to pry open the steel braces barricading my mind. I retrieved from our shelves a Bible I'd bought on a whim in college over a decade before. Dust coated the burgundy cover, and the spine literally cracked upon its first opening. Its weight in my lap felt new and strange.

I began reading in the late morning, pen in hand, winter sun streaming in, curled in an armchair after a post-call nap and a shower. Upon Scott's recommendation, I read the four Gospel accounts, then the book of Romans.

By the time I pulled myself away, the January sun had slunk below the horizon, unfurling scrolls of rose and lilac across the sky. Night found me in the same chair, staring into the dark, my heart swelling.

He died for us, I thought over and over. *God knows our suffering. He sent his Son to die and release us from it, and to save us from the punishment we're due—even though we don't deserve it. God loves us that much.*

I turned a light on again, and read and reread Romans 5:

Therefore, since we have been justified by faith, we have peace with God through our Lord Jesus Christ. Through him we have also obtained access by faith into this grace in which we stand, and we rejoice in hope of the glory of God. Not only that, but we rejoice in our sufferings, knowing that suffering produces endurance, and endurance produces character, and character produces hope, and hope does not put us to shame, because God's love has been poured into our hearts through the Holy Spirit who has been given to us.

> For while we were still weak, at the right time Christ died for the ungodly. For one will scarcely die for a righteous person—though perhaps for a good person one would dare even to die—but God shows his love for us in that while we were still sinners, Christ died for us. (Rom. 5:1–8)

The God who wove together the threads of matter became *one of us*. He humbled himself, choosing a manger for his bed when he was entitled to a throne. He healed and prayed for those who persecuted him (Luke 22:51; 23:34). He, too, endured misery and torture and the sinister, malevolent thrashings of evil. And he bore such afflictions *for us*, so that his vast love could overcome time and space to penetrate our feeble hearts.

Illness, pain, and death are the detestable fruits of the fall, and they daily break us in two. But in Christ, we have hope. He suffered too. He knows. He bore our wounds to achieve the greatest feat the world has ever witnessed: the restoration of sinful, corrupt, fallen humanity to our heavenly Father. While tragedies devastate us now, *our tears will not flow forever*. He has conquered the evil that spawns our pain. When he returns, the fruits of sin—the gunshot wounds, the brain injury, the mourning, the despondency atop bridges—will vanish from the face of the earth forever.

In Christ, God claims you for his own. Even when despair wraps vice-like around your heart, it cannot tear you from his love. It cannot rip from you your status as God's adopted child. "For I am sure that neither death nor life, nor angels nor rulers, nor things present nor things to come, nor powers, nor height nor depth, nor anything else in all creation, will be able to separate us from the love of God in Christ Jesus our Lord" (Rom. 8:38–39).

This side of the fall, when sin seethes across the globe, questions torment us in the night. We grit our teeth against pain. We sink into melancholy.

But no question, pain, or gloom can undo what Christ has accomplished. He died for us. He was raised again. Through this gospel, he offers a glimmer of hope unlike any the world has seen.

And this hope, the afterglow of God's love, strengthens us when our efforts fail, and lends meaning to what we cannot understand.

16

This Is My Blood

*And he took a cup, and when he had given thanks
he gave it to them, saying, "Drink of it, all of you,
for this is my blood of the covenant, which is poured
out for many for the forgiveness of sins."*

MATTHEW 26:27–28

SHE ARRIVED ON a stretcher encircled by paramedics. The emergency medicine attending surveyed the scene from the doorway, his arms across his chest, his expression grave. After a moment of observation, he leaned toward me. "She looks like she's bleeding out," he said.

Even I, a naive trainee at the time, could see he was right. Blood loss declared itself on her very skin. Her face was ashen, her hands cool. Sweat beaded her hairline. She breathed in deep, rapid gasps, and monitoring revealed a heart rate twice normal. When we called her name, she barely lifted her eyelids.

Her blood volume was draining away. If we didn't act quickly, her life would follow.

The Blood Is the Life

"The blood is the life" (Deut. 12:23). So Moses reminded the Israelites on the eve of his death, as he urged them to love God with all their heart, soul, and might (Deut. 6:5). His intent was to guide his people to observe Israel's dietary laws (Lev. 17:10–11), but anyone who has witnessed bleeding can affirm the truth of his declaration.

When blood loss occurs slowly, as in chronic anemia, your energy dwindles. Climbing stairs exhausts you. You feel dizzy with the slightest exertion, and want only to lie down, perhaps to sleep. You prod your muscles to perform work that once seemed automatic, but they refuse to comply.

When bleeding occurs suddenly, the effect is more dramatic. Panic seizes you. You shiver, the room spins, and nausea swamps you. You know you need help, but can barely piece words together through your chattering teeth. You feel as if life is shrinking away from you, and you're powerless to block its retreat.

The critical importance of blood in sustaining life reflects God's mastery in design. Although colored corn syrup masquerades as blood in the movies, its only similarity with the fluid in our vessels is its appearance. Human blood isn't sludgy or homogeneous, but rather a highly complex system, meticulously calibrated to support every organ in the body. Microscopy permits us a window into this world, revealing that God's majesty, so apparent in the vast, star-sprayed limbs of the galaxies, announces itself with equal fervor in the hollows of our own veins.

We owe our abilities to ponder a math problem, hug a child, taste a decadent mousse, and dash after a runaway ball to blood, surging with each heartbeat, dispersing life-giving oxygen while our thoughts turn elsewhere. Although water constitutes over 90 percent of our blood volume, *trillions* of red blood cells drift in that sea, each binding, shuttling, and releasing oxygen throughout the body. A protein on the surface of a single red cell assumes the perfect configuration to secure four oxygen molecules, then unseats them when it encounters tissues high in carbon dioxide. Through this cycle of binding, transporting, and releasing, blood continuously delivers oxygen to the organs that need it most. That oxygen, in turn, is essential for cells to fuel every reaction required for life. When the flow of blood slows, our organs falter. Processes grind to a halt. Tissues turn ashen, then blacken. When blood fails, life cannot be.

Yet even this crucial interplay between red blood cells and oxygen doesn't tell the entire story. God has designed our blood vessels as a system of byways, with blood as the medium for delivery. Medications, nutrients, and hormones all course through our arteries. White blood cells travel along this vast network to attack invading bacteria and viruses. Clotting factors and platelets in the blood stop bleeding. Even the precise concentrations of salts in our bloodstream are essential, supporting the brain and heart when balanced, triggering seizures and cardiac arrest when spun off-kilter. Anyone admitted to the hospital has undergone blood draws upon arrival to the ER, or early in the morning before the doctors arrive, or in haste by a frantic intern, because harbingers of our wellness and sickness, recovery and decline, all lurk within the blood.

Our own medical capabilities pale in comparison to this elegant system. As mentioned in chapter 3, we can neither reproduce nor perfectly replace lost blood. Instead, we rely upon donated blood that we separate into fractions, mix with preservatives, and refrigerate. If you've ever received a transfusion or cared for someone bleeding, perhaps you've handled these chilled plastic parcels and have witnessed their mediocre effects compared with the lifeblood pulsing through our veins. Too many transfusions of red cells, without commensurate doses of clotting factors, and we actually bleed more. Cut surfaces and IV puncture sites begin to ooze, and the blood thins to the consistency of water. Our potassium and acid levels can rise too high and our calcium levels dive too low, threatening nerves, the heart, and their constituent enzymes. Transfused blood stuns our immune cells, deforming them until they lodge in capillaries. The marvel surging through our veins is critical for life, yet so complex and ingenious that we can barely approximate its effects.

We owe our abilities to run, dream, love, laugh, write a sentence, and catch a football to our blood.

We owe our standing before a holy God as beloved, cherished, renewed, washed clean, and righteous, to Christ's.

The Blood Makes Atonement

Ever since the garden, we've owed God our lifeblood. The sacrificial system from the Old Testament might strike our modern ears as brutal, but it was an extension of God's mercy, upholding justice while offering the Israelites an avenue for repentance. "The wages of sin is death" (Rom. 6:23), and without God's sovereign grace, those wages would swallow us up as penalty for our sins. "For the life of the flesh is in the blood," the Lord tells Moses in Leviticus 17:11, "and I have given it for you on the altar to make atonement for your souls, for it is the blood that makes atonement by the life." In the letter to the Hebrews, we read, "Indeed, under the law almost everything is purified with blood, and without the shedding of blood there is no forgiveness of sins" (Heb. 9:22). Sin disgraces the souls of all mankind, but even in the days of the patriarchs, God paved a road to forgiveness: an animal's blood on the altar, in place of theirs.

In the book of Exodus, God saved his people through that same sacrificial blood upon their doorposts. When the angel of death swept over Egypt, the blood of a lamb "without blemish" spared God's people (Ex. 12:5). "The blood shall be a sign for you, on the houses where you are," we read in Exodus 12:13. "And when I see the blood, I will pass over you, and no plague will befall you to destroy you, when I strike the land of Egypt." In obedience to God's command, the Israelites would observe the Passover for generations afterward (Ex. 12:14), to remember that "on that very day the LORD brought the people of Israel out of the land of Egypt by their hosts" (Ex. 12:51). The blood of the lamb, who died in their place, conferred mercy and life to God's enslaved people. The mark upon their doorways secured for them the fruits of God's grace.

The blood of the lamb set them free.

This Is My Blood

God's provision for his people during the exodus foreshadowed the greater exodus (Luke 9:31), accomplished millennia later in Jerusalem. God saved the firstborn sons of Israel at the Passover. After another Passover meal, he would give his own firstborn Son to save the entire world. "For God so loved the world, that he gave his only Son, that whoever believes in him should not perish but have eternal life" (John 3:16).

Jesus is the true sacrificial Lamb. During the exodus, the blood of unblemished lambs saved God's people from imminent death and freed them from oppression. On the cross, Christ's blood saved us from permanent death and liberated us from our bondage to sin

(John 8:34–36). Jesus himself, while sharing the Passover meal with those dearest to him, with his own harrowing death encroaching, declared himself the one who would lay down his life to give us life everlasting: "And he took a cup, and when he had given thanks he gave it to them, saying, 'Drink of it, all of you, for this is my blood of the covenant, which is poured out for many for the forgiveness of sins'" (Matt. 26:27–28).

Jesus bled in our place, giving his life "as a ransom for many" (Matt. 20:28). He was the unblemished Lamb, perfectly obedient to the Father in life, and the perfect fulfillment of Old Testament prophesy in death, with even the integrity of his bones a sign of God's realized promises: "But when they came to Jesus and saw that he was already dead, they did not break his legs. . . . For these things took place that the Scripture might be fulfilled: 'Not one of his bones will be broken'" (John 19:33, 36; Ps. 34:20). God's own Son gave his life freely, for us, to rescue us from the grisly fate our sins earn us. He offered up his own blood for our doorposts. As Peter writes, "You were ransomed from the futile ways inherited from your forefathers, not with perishable things such as silver or gold, but with the precious blood of Christ, like that of a lamb without blemish or spot" (1 Pet. 1:18–19).

Jesus poured out his own life-giving blood for us, to anoint us with eternal life.

What Wondrous Love Is This

How astounding is the love of God for us, that he would conde-scend to walk among us? How wondrous, that the one through whom the skies and seas were created, would humble himself to lay his hands upon us? How awe-inspiring is our God that his Son, the radiance of his glory (Heb. 1:3), would so shower us with mercy as to shed his own blood where ours is due? And with what exultation can we rejoice, knowing that through his blood, we are healed! "For if the blood of goats and bulls, and the sprinkling of defiled persons with the ashes of a heifer, sanctify for the purification of the flesh, how much more will the blood of Christ, who through the eternal Spirit offered himself without blemish to God, purify our conscience from dead works to serve the living God" (Heb. 9:13–14).

When a needle prick awakens you for the hundredth time in the dead of night, and you wince at the sting when warmth ebbs from you to fill a synthetic tube, remember the precious blood of Christ. For "we have redemption through his blood, the forgiveness of our trespasses, according to the riches of his grace" (Eph. 1:7).

When in caring for others you hang yet another transfusion of packed red blood cells, or hold pressure on a wound to stop the bleeding, gather courage from what God has done through Christ: "For in him all the fullness of God was pleased to dwell, and through him to reconcile to himself all things, whether on earth or in heaven, making peace by the blood of his cross" (Col. 1:19–20).

The blood flowing within you churns up life so you might breathe, think, and love. But the blood of the Lamb, poured out for you, blesses you with life everlasting.

Heavenly Father, you orchestrate the ebb and flow of life within us. As you infuse our blood with life, so also you gave your Son, so that in his blood we might be cleansed, clothed in his righteousness before you. We praise you and thank you that you so loved us as to send your only Son, the unblemished Lamb, to free us with his precious blood. All glory and honor be yours, forever and ever! Amen.

17

Called Out of the Darkness

But you are a chosen race, a royal priesthood, a holy
nation, a people for his own possession, that you
may proclaim the excellencies of him who called
you out of darkness into his marvelous light.

1 PETER 2:9

WHEN HE ARRIVED in the ER, his skin was the color of an oyster, his lips blue. He barely responded to a shout of his name or a rub of his chest. He was a young man in the prime of his life, and he was in shock.

He was a professional skier. During a competition he was favored to win, he lost control on the downslope, plunged thirty feet off course, and rolled like tumbleweed down a hill until a tree trunk broke his fall. When paramedics found him, he denied any pain, but repeated over and over, his voice taut with panic, that he couldn't move his limbs.

The trauma bay came alive as we worked to save his life. We placed a tube into his windpipe and another into his chest to re-expand the lung that had collapsed like a rumpled shopping bag. A catheter threaded into his wrist offered a conduit for blood draws and monitoring. More catheters served as entryways for fluid and medications, which we poured in to urge his blood volume to swell and his vessels to constrict.

Gradually his skin flushed, and his extremities warmed. His oxygen levels and blood pressure rose to values supportive of life. Our shoulders relaxed just a bit, and our own breathing slowed.

Yet this young man's challenges were far from over. A CT scan confirmed what we'd feared: the accident had smashed his spinal column at the level of the neck. Like blocks sliding past each other, the upper vertebra slid forward, compressing his spinal cord, threatening to sever it if we didn't repair the fractures. The bustle resumed as neurosurgeons rushed him to the operating room.

Days later, he lay in an ICU bed with metal screws and rods fixing his spinal column into place. The tubes from his mouth and chest were gone, and he could converse freely. The threat to his life had passed.

But he didn't rejoice. While we'd saved his life, we couldn't save his spinal cord, and he remained paralyzed from the shoulders down. Hour after hour he stared at the ceiling, his face expressionless, his affect blunted, with his limbs useless and limp upon the bed. When we examined him each morning, he'd answer "yes" or "no," but said little else.

Then one day, his nurse motioned for us to talk with her in private. She looked stricken.

"I offered to brush his teeth, and he suddenly burst into tears," she said. "He says everything he cares about is gone. I mean, can you blame him? He was a professional skier, right? But I don't know what to do, or how to help him. He says he doesn't know who he is anymore."

I Am Lost

Although few experiences are as devastating as quadriplegia, outbursts like that of this young man echo in every hospital hallway. When an accident or sudden illness assails us, our first prayers are for our survival. In desperation we plead with the Lord to save us, to use our doctors to win us more days on this earth. When we survive, we gush with gratitude.

In time, however, the dust settles. We stare dumbfounded at our strange surroundings, and realize that the lives through which we once absentmindedly strolled have disintegrated. The images we took for granted have burned up, their edges curling, the elements of ourselves we most highly prized crumbling into ash.

You may have braved such an upheaval in life. Perhaps you survived a stroke, but can no longer walk. Or you persevered through seemingly endless complications after surgery, only to return home dependent upon a catheter for nutrition, never again indulging in the tastes that evoke treasured memories of home. You might have undergone a joint replacement, then spent months learning how to walk again. Your body might be daily quivering and faltering, your very muscles and bones barring you from basic joys that instill life with meaning. Meanwhile, you still yearn to go fishing again, or to stroll beside the sea, or to lift a sticky-cheeked toddler into your arms. You still yearn to engage in the pursuits that have shaped you.

In such moments we can lose sight of who we are. Disability, just as it impairs us physically, also cripples the spirit. In the most dramatic cases, as with the young man who'd survived his crash on a ski slope, the realization that life has changed occurs suddenly. The effect is rapid, violent, like the ripping open of a wound. The anesthesia wears off, we shed tears of relief that we've survived for another sunrise, and then the weight of our circumstances crushes us.

At other times, we lose ourselves gradually, the way mist slowly obliterates a path.

David stumbled through that fog during his last year. Over a period of months, he progressed from needing inhalers occasionally, to requiring oxygen around the clock, to losing his ability to climb even a few stairs. Initially, he accepted these setbacks positively, and pointed, as was his gifting, to God's goodness and mercy in all things. Yet as missed moments sank into a permanent pattern, gradually sadness drew over him like a sheet. When he admitted he could no longer climb our front steps for monthly dinners with our family or commit to sharing his testimony with the congregation, grief tinged his words. Then, when he had to give up teaching his small group halfway through their study of the book of Acts, his regret hardened into resentment. His very identity seemed to fray, and he wrestled with questions of his purpose in a hectic world that he could no longer navigate.

David wasn't alone in this experience. Imprinted on my memory are the cries of a woman for whom I cared in medical school as she curled on her bed and pleaded for help. The arteries in her legs had calcified so severely that she suffered from continuous, unrelenting pain, and her toes had blackened from poor blood flow. She needed bilateral amputations.

Every day, she refused surgery. She had no other option for relief, but the idea of losing her legs, and forever banishing her hope of walking through the New York streets that had defined her life since girlhood, distressed her even more than the searing pain that kept her awake all night. From sunset until dawn, she would lie with her legs pulled to her chest, rubbing her dying feet and moaning. Then in the morning when our team visited her, she pleaded with us not to take those shriveled, burning legs from her.

Then there was the woman who lost her vision after an accident, and in follow-up, lamented that with her dependence on others for things she took for granted—cooking a meal, going to the grocery store, paying bills—she felt like she'd lost a vital part of herself. Or the singer whose thyroid cancer we'd cured, but who suffered a nerve injury that paralyzed one of her vocal cords, transforming her bell-like soprano into a raspy croak. Or the woman whose joy over the birth of her first child was trampled by hemorrhage after her C-section. Her complaint of lightheadedness progressed to shortness of breath, and ultimately her bleeding escalated so out of control that she required an emergency hysterectomy to save her life. She awoke with her life spared, and with her new baby squirming and flushed beside her, but the reality that she would never bear children again gutted her.

All such examples capture the power of medical crises to threaten our understanding of who we are. We may escape a health catastrophe with our lives, but every disaster leaves a mark. Some scars we can plaster over and then move on. Others so disfigure us that we no longer recognize ourselves. We float, dazed, through the wreckage of our lives, and wonder where to find meaning in the debris. Like Jeremiah stumbling through the ruins of Jerusalem, we cry out, "I am lost" (Lam. 3:54).

Called Out of the Darkness

When you look with dread upon the pieces of your fractured life, know that your worth derives from something far more permanent, far more precious, than these scattered fragments. "For the LORD sees not as man sees: man looks on the outward appearance, but the LORD looks on the heart" (1 Sam. 16:7).

God's love for you doesn't diminish if you require a wheelchair, or if you need help to get to the doctor or to pay your bills. He isn't troubled by your sudden inability to navigate your house, or your new reliance upon others for the basics of living. While you reel in the face of a life contorted beyond recognition, mourning the confidence you once wielded and the person you thought you were, he still sees you as his beloved image bearer, made new in Christ.

Your worth doesn't derive from your self-reliance, your talents, or your independence. You can't earn it via anything your trembling hands accomplish. Rather, your worth springs solely, wholly, beautifully, and immutably, from Jesus. His blood, for yours. Your renewal, caught up in his. Your true and foremost identity has nothing to do with the vigor of your limbs or the keenness of your eyesight and everything to do with the truth that you are *an image bearer of God, loved by God and made new through Christ.*

Consider the words of Peter:

> You are a chosen race, a royal priesthood, a holy nation, a people for his own possession, that you may proclaim the excellencies of him who called you out of darkness into his marvelous light. Once you were not a people, but now you are God's people; once you had not received mercy, but now you have received mercy. (1 Pet. 2:9–10)

This is the reality of who you are: "called out of darkness, into his marvelous light." The Light of the world has called you to dwell in his radiance. In Christ you are redeemed, "created after the likeness of God in true righteousness and holiness"

(Eph. 4:24). When God looks upon you, even in your lameness, even when you cannot recognize yourself, he doesn't see someone grasping at an identity shaped by the world. Instead, he sees righteousness and holiness. He sees a reflection of his own marvelous light.

In Christ, when God looks at you, he sees his Son.

Like sunlight flooding a long-forgotten room, this truth chases away all the shadows that displace God from our hearts. You may be a spouse, a mother, a father. You may be a lawyer, a teacher, a bus driver. But first and foremost, in Christ you are a child of God. Paul writes, "In love, he predestined us for adoption to himself as sons through Jesus Christ, according to the purpose of his will, to the praise of his glorious grace, with which he has blessed us in the Beloved" (Eph. 1:4–6).

Cleave to this truth, as steps you took for granted decades earlier now feel like labor. Revel in it, when the person you envisioned yourself to be seems a distant memory. When the days unfold before you like a path plunging into the fog, the destination hazy, the journey bleak, dare to rejoice that all identifiers shrink before *who you are in Christ*. Revisit John's declaration: "See what kind of love the Father has given to us, that we should be called children of God; and so we are" (1 John 3:1).

As a follower of Christ your identity, now and forever, is as one called out of the darkness into his holy light. Jesus said, "I am the light of the world. Whoever follows me will not walk in darkness, but will have the light of life" (John 8:12). By that light, you conform to the image of God's Son. By that light, God wraps you in his love. And nothing, not illness or death, not halting speech or a crippled limb, can snuff that light out or shroud you from its brilliance (Rom. 8:38–39).

18

Living Water

*Whoever drinks of the water that I will give him will never
be thirsty again. The water that I will give him will become
in him a spring of water welling up to eternal life.*

JOHN 4:14

IN 1972, ASTRONAUTS en route to the moon aboard the Apollo
17 spacecraft photographed the earth in full sunlight. In the image,
Madagascar peeks from beneath swirls of cloud, while the horn
of Africa and the Arabian peninsula clench together like a jaw. A
cyclone drifts off the coast of India, and Antarctica locks the south
pole in a plate of ice.

This view of our mighty continents as suddenly finite and fragile
inspires awe, and it sparked an entire movement in environmental
awareness. Yet the title of the photograph reflects none of these
marvels of land and sky. Instead, this famous picture is called "The
Blue Marble," a name that highlights Earth's vast oceans glowing
blue in the void, proclaiming our most precious resource.

Although water covers 71 percent of the earth's surface, only a
tiny fraction of this volume is drinkable. Nearly 97 percent of the

earth's water fills the oceans, supporting countless species of flora and fauna, yet offering us little fresh water to sustain our lives.[1] Most people in the world collect their daily water from rivers, yet these constitute only one millionth of the water on the planet. Two-thirds of the fresh water necessary for our survival lurks in glaciers, and another 30 percent dwells underground.

Meanwhile, our very lives depend on the availability of fresh water, because we are *made* of water. Two-thirds of our body weight is water, most of it filling our cells, the rest gliding in the spaces between them. Fluid maintains just the right blood pressure to supply oxygen to our organs. It lubricates our joints, regulates our body temperature, and cushions our brain. Our every cell relies upon a steady supply of water—two to three liters each day for the average person—because without enough, everything shuts down. Our kidneys fail, disrupting the balance of electrolytes. Our liver fails, and our blood clotting deteriorates. While we can survive without food for weeks, without water we die in just three days.

My Soul Thirsts

Anyone frequenting the hospital has glimpsed the centrality of water to life. Amniotic fluid ushers in birth. Tears dampen our cheeks. In severe illness, our capillaries leak fluid that balloons our limbs.

For a vast array of conditions, the first therapy in the hospital involves the prick of a needle, connection to silicone tubing, and the infusion of a bag of fluid, essentially water with a handful of

---

1   "How Much Water Is There on Earth?" USGS.com, accessed January 14, 2020, https://www.usgs.gov/special-topic/water-science-school/science/how-much-water-there-earth?qt-science_center_objects=0#qt-science_center_objects.

salts. Such fluids restore life-giving blood flow in myriad cases, from pancreatitis to toxic shock syndrome, and from diabetic coma to diverticulitis.

Yet even when bags of fluid empty into us, swelling our cells with plenty, we thirst. We require water for every spark and reaction of life, but even the brisk bolus of fluid, the clink of ice in a glass, or the shimmer of a freshwater lake cannot slake our longing for God. He formed us to know him, glorify him, and enjoy him, but our sins cut us off from his ever-flowing love. Our parched hearts crack. They crumble and cough dust in our yearning for God, and we take up David's cry, "As a deer pants for flowing streams, so pants my soul for you, O God. My soul thirsts for God, for the living God" (Ps. 42:1–2).

Water from the Rock

During the exodus, the Israelites enjoyed an unprecedented proximity to the living God. God spoke with Abraham and wrestled with Jacob, but during the flight from Egypt God *dwelt among* his people, guiding them through the wilderness and safeguarding them with his power. His faithfulness materialized in columns of fire and smoke: "And the LORD went before them by day in a pillar of cloud to lead them along the way, and by night in a pillar of fire to give them light, that they might travel by day and by night. The pillar of cloud by day and the pillar of fire by night did not depart from before the people" (Ex. 13:21–22). When the Israelites encamped at Sinai, God himself then tabernacled with them (Ex. 25:21–22). As he ushered them toward freedom, God gave the Israelites the very gift for which we all yearn: communion with him, a life bound up in his goodness and his loving provision.

Yet the Israelites' fallen, sinful hearts, so like our own, would not be satisfied. While encamped at Rephidim, they preoccupied themselves with their own dry throats, dismissed God's covenantal promises, and exchanged praise for griping: "But the people thirsted there for water, and the people grumbled against Moses and said, 'Why did you bring us up out of Egypt, to kill us and our children and our livestock with thirst?'" (Ex. 17:3).

Given all they'd witnessed—the Nile turned to blood, the sun darkened, all their enemies swept into the waters (Ex. 15:21)—the Israelites' complaints reflected not just ingratitude, but a corrupting, penetrating unbelief. As their idolatry of the golden calf at the foot of Mount Sinai would prove (Ex. 32:1–6), they still placed their faith in the works of their own hands, rather than in the Lord who unshackled those hands from slavery. This was sin at its most fundamental: faith turned inward, toward the self, rather than lifted to the Lord of heaven and earth.

"The wages of sin is death" (Rom. 6:23), and in his perfect righteousness, holiness, and justice, God could have raised his hand in wrath against the Israelites and struck them down. At first, as God talked with Moses in Exodus 17, it seemed judgment was precisely his plan: "So Moses cried to the LORD, 'What shall I do with this people? They are almost ready to stone me.' And the LORD said to Moses, 'Pass on before the people, taking with you some of the elders of Israel, and take in your hand the staff with which you struck the Nile, and go'" (Ex. 17:4–5).

The staff God commanded Moses to take up is the same rod of judgment he raised against hard-hearted Pharaoh. With it, Moses struck the Nile, and as punishment for Pharaoh's wickedness the river's life-giving waters soured to blood. Given this history, when we read that God told Moses to "take in your hand the staff," we ready ourselves for a similar account of divine judgment.

Then, something remarkable happened. God didn't command Moses to strike down the people. Instead, he commanded Moses to strike *him*: "Behold, I will stand before you there on the rock at Horeb, and you shall strike the rock, and water shall come out of it, and the people will drink" (Ex. 17:6).

Moses does as the Lord instructs. Rather than punish his idolatrous people, with his staff Moses strikes *God himself*, there upon the rock. Then the rock yields its water, and the people drink and are refreshed.

The God for whom we all thirst *took on the punishment* his people deserved. He bore their judgment and provided water to restore them in an arid wasteland. While they grumbled and dismissed his mercies, he made himself the rock that would bear the rod, so they might have water to replenish their weary souls.

And Christ, that rock in the desert, pours out water for us as well, welling up to eternal life.

In his first letter to the church at Corinth, Paul unpacks this scene from the exodus: "For they drank from the spiritual Rock that followed them, and the Rock was Christ" (1 Cor. 10:4). The one who braced against the staff and poured out water so others might live was Christ. Just as Christ bore the penalty the Israelites deserved in the desert, so also he suffered wrath once and for all for us.

We can't procure the water for which we all yearn. We can't dig for it, or bail it. We can't build that well, pump it, strive or scheme for it. We can't even acquire it through an IV bag, or a plunge into the ocean, or a cool cup of water in a beaded glass on a sweltering day.

It comes only by God's grace, by the fissure in the Rock, split open for our sins, issuing forth life.

Living Water

Water supports every flicker and spark of molecules in our bodies. We search the heavens for water, because without it life cannot thrive. Yet the water that envelopes the earth and fills our bodies still can't give us the life that Jesus offers. The water of this world sustains for a time, but its wells drain dry, its founts diminish to a trickle. The water within us vanishes into the air as we breathe. After half a day without water, our tongues stick to the roof of our mouths, and like the Israelites in the wilderness, we groan in thirst. We drink, and are briefly satisfied, but too quickly our thirst returns.

Christ, in contrast, offers us living water, a spring welling up to eternal life (John 4:10, 14). The water that sprang from the Rock also flows through the New Jerusalem: "the river of the water of life, bright as crystal, flowing from the throne of God and of the Lamb" (Rev. 22:1). It runs freely, its source never depleted, buoying us to everlasting life. As Jesus said to the Samaritan woman at the well, "Everyone who drinks of this water will be thirsty again, but whoever drinks of the water that I will give him will never be thirsty again" (John 4:13–14).

Christ satisfies our most desperate thirst. When in the middle of the night your mouth feels like sand and you plead for a swab, or when you glance up at a bag of saline hovering over you, or when you scrub your palms beneath the water once more to wash them clean, remember the one who offers us living water. When we grumble and groan, he takes our unbelief upon himself. He bears the penalty we deserve. And through the crack in that rock, he gives us eternal life that will never ebb, that will never recede, that in waves of mercy carries us into the arms of God.

Heavenly Father, as thirst burns within us, we rejoice that through Christ you pour out living water, a wellspring to eternal life that will never dry up. When our throats scorch, help us to cleave to the grace manifest in your Son. Help us to remember the Rock who has taken our punishment, such that the rivers of your grace carry us toward you. In Jesus's name we pray. Amen.

19

I Will Give You Rest

Come to me, all who labor and are heavy laden, and I will
give you rest. Take my yoke upon you, and learn from me,
for I am gentle and lowly in heart, and you will find rest for
your souls. For my yoke is easy, and my burden is light.

MATTHEW 11:28–30

AFTER HE REMEMBERED Isaiah 6, David knew that God was
near, and that he was sovereign over all the mess. He knew he was
forgiven in Christ, and that when he drew his last breath he'd be
with his Savior.

Yet while he found assurance in the gospel, the *process* of death
still frightened him. A dear friend of his had died alone, and as he
considered his own diminishing days, her memory haunted him.
"I'm not scared of where I'm going," he'd say. "I'm scared of going
through it. I don't want to die in pain. And I especially don't want
to die alone."

For months, I worried that a painful, lonely death was exactly
what awaited him. For half a year David required more and more
intensive interventions while in the hospital, and was able to cope

out of the hospital for shorter and shorter periods of time. His body was slowly falling apart, incapable of functioning without the aid of machines. With every hospitalization things got worse.

Unfortunately, in our overtaxed and fragmented medical system, no one surveyed the trajectory of his illness and engaged him in the hard conversations. Most clinicians attended to him until his breathing shakily stabilized, then discharged him, with no procedure or supports in place to rescue him when his scarred lungs inevitably failed again. He couldn't afford home health services or assisted living, so he was cast back out, alone and without help, to promptly decompensate again.

With David's permission, I urged his physicians to formulate a prognosis, and to devise a plan for him more reliable than a call to 911 when friends happened to discover him unconscious. At first the conversations seemed to help, but then David transferred to a rehabilitation center, where the task was punted to another team. They, in turn, deferred to the hospital—and an entirely new care team—when he worsened again. David suspected he was dying, but in our era of superspecialized care, no one confirmed his intuition, or offered to guide him through the days ahead.

The constant stress and inconsistencies took a toll on David. He oscillated between resignation that his life was ending, and dogged determination to press on. On days when he was lucid, he would call friends and loved ones to voice the things on his heart, and select hymns and verses for his funeral. Then in a reversal, one day he changed his code status from "do not resuscitate" (DNR) to "full code," stating, "I want every doctor within a hundred miles pounding on my chest!" Caught in the maelstrom of illness he grasped at the rudder, thrashing one way before fear lurched him back in the opposite direction.

Meanwhile, he continued to decline. His intervals of wellness gradually dwindled to nothing. Paranoia and delirium set in, provoking David to launch bizarre accusations at his nurses. He saw giant flashing objects whirling about his room. While he once doled out Bibles to the cleaning staff, he now eyed the janitor warily, suspecting him of some unvoiced foul play.

As I watched him worsen, David's future troubled me daily. A death alone and in pain seemed precisely the destiny for my beloved brother, my friend who so loved the Lord. *Please, Lord*, I prayed over and over. *Please protect him. Let your grace rain down.*

Weary and Burdened

One day during his last hospitalization, for no obvious reason, David's delirium cleared. His thinking was logical and rational. The waking nightmares vanished.

That very same morning, after all the days he'd struggled in a hospital bed without guidance, two crucial things happened. First, one of his doctors told him his prognosis: he had stage-four COPD, and was at the end of life. Second, in the wake of this prognosis, a palliative care specialist determined he was eligible for hospice.

Understandably, at first David reacted with anger. "Why didn't anyone tell me before?" he railed. "Why were you all hiding this from me?" Gradually, though, his temper softened, and he listened to his options. Further aggressive care wasn't going to help him, as it hadn't for six months. No treatment or ventilator could reverse the damage that had eaten away his lungs. He was dying, and no treatment could bring him back to the life he loved. Nothing we could do could stave off death.

After a long discussion, David chose hospice care. It offered the best chance of meaningful moments with friends and family, away from the machines and mind-altering medications that would never heal him.

When I heard the news I cried. *Thank you, Lord. Thank you, Jesus.*

Like a curtain falling over his mind, delirium descended upon David again that afternoon. The moment of clarity, during which so much had been decided and so much grace shown, came and went. My kids and I brought him a box of fried chicken, and he slept for most of our visit, a noninvasive ventilator mask blasting every few seconds to push air into his honeycombed lungs. Even my young children could plainly see that he'd worsened. He would flutter his eyes open, but didn't acknowledge them. No jokes or stories about cartoon characters came. His few comments, usually about the janitor outside or the nurse overnight, rang sharp with suspicion. As we left, I texted his sister, who was en route to visit him: "He's paranoid," I wrote. "Please don't be upset by his words. It's the disease, not him."

After we left the hospital, I took the kids on a hike in the woods near our home. The trees were in bud, and the oaks and birches lit up the forest in spring green. We walked along muddy trails, my kids racing ahead, I lingering behind in my grief. At a vernal pool the kids paused to throw sticks into the water, and I took in the air and color. Clouds sailed like ships through an endless sea. Peepers and wood frogs chorused as the wind picked up. I scanned the water, its surface a mirror, and searched for the frogs I couldn't see, but whose presence I knew by their voices.

It all seemed so remote from the machines and pale corridors that entrapped my dear friend. Yet the beauty offered a bittersweet reminder of God's love. Remnants of his life-giving breath flourished even while the dying groaned in houses of pain. The winds fluttered on. His creation still sang. He was ever present, never changing. And he was waiting to wrap David in his splendor.

"What are you looking at, Mum?" my six-year-old son Jack asked, a birch branch in his grubby hand.

"Just all the beauty."

"Ah, yes," he said. "I love God's world."

My Yoke Is Easy

That night, after I prayed with him before bedtime, Jack filled the dark with questions.

"Is Mr. David going to heaven, Mum?"

"He most certainly is, buddy. It's so sad that he's dying, but we know he'll be with Jesus."

"When Jesus comes back, will Mr. David have pink lungs?"

"Yes, sweetie, he will."

"Why do people get old?"

"Our bodies just fall apart over time."

"Why do our bodies fall apart?"

"It's because of sin, honey. We all eventually die."

He fell quiet, although in the deepening dark I could tell his mind raced. Finally, he choked back a sob.

"Mum, can we please see Mr. David every day, until he dies? I want to see him every day."

I will be forever grateful to God for working through the heart of our little boy that night. He discerned wisdom I could not (Matt. 11:25).

We had a list of obligations to manage the next day, but we cancelled everything to come alongside our dying brother. We arrived at the hospice center to find David brighter than we'd seen him in weeks. He sat with his laptop open to a letter he wanted read at his funeral, that he was insistent upon finishing without help.

"Look at this place!" he exclaimed when we entered. "I'm a prince here. I never want to leave!" He pointed to the beautiful tree-lined pathway winding beyond his atrium windows. "I'm thinking I'll take a walk outside later."

An aide interrupted to take his lunch order. When she told him he could have anything he wanted, his mouth dropped in disbelief. After months of a restrictive hospital diet, most of the food barely edible, the prospect of choice in a meal floored him. Almost timidly, he asked for a ham-and-cheese sandwich on a roll, with a double serving of mayonnaise. When she returned with the sandwich, I thought he might kiss her.

We chatted about church, friends, and family, the sort of banter we used to share so long ago over homemade stir fry at the kitchen table, before ventilators and breathing treatments became fixtures in life. My daughter, Christie, usually silent during our visits, suddenly opened up in conversation, which surprised and delighted him. He mentioned his bucket list: to attend church once more, to celebrate another Christmas with family, to give his testimony one last time. Then he lapsed into a long moment of silence, his gaze cast toward the sun-bathed pathway outside.

"The moments for which I've been most grateful have been when someone has unexpectedly come to visit me," he finally said. "I'm always so shocked someone would take time to see me, and so grateful to God for that gift."

I fought against tears. "That you say this, is exactly why you're such a gift to us. You have the most beautiful ability to give God praise in all things, from great to small, no matter what's happening."

He took in the words, held onto them. We sat in silence for a while. Then his shoulders sagged. Fatigue seemed to creep upon him again. I thought about his letter awaiting completion, and how much it mattered to him.

"We'd better get going, and let you finish," I said. "We'll come visit tomorrow, okay?" I rose to my feet, and gave him a hug, as did both the kids. "We love you."

As we left, Jack blurted, "See you later, alligator!" David laughed, and echoed the line back to him.

The joke would be the last words we would hear him say this side of heaven.

Come to Me

David fell unconscious the next morning. Instead of racing him back to the hospital to endure another barrage of futile treatments, the staff focused on keeping him peaceful.

Those of us blessed to call him our brother took turns at his side. All day we held his hand and talked to him, reminiscing about the times we'd treasured together. Our pastor visited for hours, and together we sang David's favorite hymn and read Romans 8 and Psalms 23, 34, and 43. We lingered, as he would have, over Psalm 34:4: "I sought the LORD, and he answered me and delivered me from all my fears." We read aloud his favorite passage, Matthew 11:28–30: "Come to me, all who labor and are heavy laden, and I will give you rest. Take my yoke upon you, and learn from me, for I am gentle and lowly in heart, and you will find rest for your souls. For my yoke is easy, and my burden is light."

When day softened into evening, we leaned over to embrace him one last time. He had been silent for hours, but when Christie hugged him, David seemed to answer, his voice suddenly renewing itself for a fleeting moment. Perhaps he heard her. Perhaps he was responding to some other call from the Lord. We will never know, but we count his reply a glimmer of grace, another gift from God to sweeten our memories.

David's older sister sat beside him throughout the night. She prayed over him and assured him that family was near, and God's love even nearer. Then in the morning, as the sun again flooded the path outside his window, his breathing, strained and hard for so long, quieted to a stop. His heartbeat soon also hushed.

We cried for the loss of our dear friend, for the hollow his absence carved in our hearts.

And we thanked the Lord for the assurance that David was in the arms of his Savior, enfolded in glory, delivered into rest for his soul.

You Will Find Rest for Your Souls

David still wanted to do so much—to share another Christmas, to return to church, to tell his story. That he couldn't is tragic. Yet his greatest fear wasn't an inability to do more in life, but rather the prospect of dying alone and in pain. And God, because he is merciful and gracious, slow to anger, and abounding in steadfast love and faithfulness (Ex. 34:6), provided for his servant, even when medicine failed him. When all circumstances seemed intent upon committing David to a death in the hospital, or alone in an apartment with no one beside him, God ordained that he would draw his last breath surrounded by family, resting, while those he loved filled his ears with God's word. As with his people in the wilderness, when "the pillar of cloud by day and the pillar of fire by night did not depart from before the people" (Ex. 13:22), so also the Lord never departed from David.

Just as he pointed to Christ in life, after his death David's legacy bore witness to God's goodness. The funeral he'd so diligently planned, even when he could barely think or breathe, included a video proclaiming God's goodness in all things and the hope we have in Christ Jesus. The hymn he chose was "Blessed Assurance":

Blessed assurance, Jesus is mine!
O what a foretaste of glory divine!
Heir of salvation, purchase of God,
born of his Spirit, washed in his blood.

This is my story, this is my song,
praising my Savior, all the day long;
this is my story, this is my song,
praising my Savior, all the day long.[1]

Our pastor read his farewell letter at the funeral service. In addition to expressing his love for friends and family, David quoted Romans 8:38–39: "For I am sure that neither death nor life, nor angels nor rulers, nor things present nor things to come, nor powers, nor height nor depth, nor anything else in all creation, will be able to separate us from the love of God in Christ Jesus our Lord." It was the same verse my husband had read to him during his last week of life, and when we received David's Bible for safekeeping, its leather cover worn from hours of reading and rereading, his bookmark was carefully placed in Romans 8. His final contemplations of God's word included the assurance that nothing could wrench him from God's love in Christ, and in his last moment on earth, he chose to share that truth, that well of hope, with others.

---

1 "Blessed Assurance," Fanny J. Crosby, 1873.

During his walk upon the earth, David endured homelessness, drug addiction, breathlessness, and the despair of a life whittled away by disease. Yet ultimately none of these hardships threatened the promise God gave him in Christ: rest for his weary soul. The world wore him down, but Christ promised an easy yoke. A light burden. A heart, mind, and body made new by God's grace, through faith alone, in Christ alone.

The effects of sin strangle us. The woes we carry crush us. But in Christ, we who labor and are heavy-burdened find rest for our souls.

20

I Will Be with You

Fear not, for I have redeemed you;
I have called you by name, you are mine.
When you pass through the waters, I will be with you;
and through the rivers, they shall not overwhelm you;
when you walk through fire you shall not be burned,
and the flame shall not consume you.
For I am the LORD your God,
the Holy One of Israel, your Savior.

ISAIAH 43:1–3

WHEN I WAS ON mission in Kenya, a boy of about ten arrived alone to our clinic. His bare feet were caked with red mud. After leaving his house at five in the morning and walking miles to reach us, he waited for two hours in a line snaking across a field to see the mysterious doctors who had traveled across the ocean.

When our staff glimpsed him, they ushered him to the front of the queue, and I immediately saw why. An abscess the size of a walnut bulged from his eyebrow. The surrounding infection had swollen his eye shut, rimming half his face in a red, angry halo.

Our clinic had plenty of Tylenol and vitamins, but we weren't equipped for surgical procedures, even those as minor as draining an abscess. Our "examination room" consisted of a wooden picnic table behind a tarp suspended from the ceiling. Yet if left undrained, the infection in this boy's face would spread behind his eye and threaten his brain. The child lived in a remote village, days away from any facility with bright lights and sterile instruments. As rudimentary as we were, we were his only option.

I had brought a sterile debridement kit, including a scalpel blade. I only had to make a small nick with the blade, a small feat compared to the challenges of the trauma bay. Still, my stomach twisted at the thought of incising this poor boy's face when he had no family with him to provide comfort. Wasn't he going through enough, with his family scratching out a living without help? As an image bearer of God, didn't he deserve the same comprehensive care we could provide in the United States?

An interpreter explained what we'd have to do, and he lay down on the table in silence, his face blank. Nurses stood on-hand to hold and console him.

I blotted on antiseptic, we gave an antibiotic and lidocaine, and after a silent prayer I drained the abscess. Pus burst forth, followed by bleeding from the wound edges. I irrigated the wound with saline and held pressure.

Throughout he remained quiet, either because courage steeled him, or because he had endured hurts and fears far worse than the scalpel blade of a foreigner. He winced at the pressure of the blade, but never cried out. He never moved, never spoke, just breathed and waited for my gloved hands, warm like his, but so unlike his own in their daily occupations, to finish their strange work.

I placed a gauze dressing and prayed the drainage would clear the infection. "Will you please come back tomorrow? To have me check the wound and change the bandage?" I urged.

He studied my face, and seemed to weigh my words as the interpreter translated them. A return trip meant another half-day walk, followed by another wait in an hours-long queue. Could he really spare another day away from helping his family with their daily work? To my relief, he said he'd return, although I knew the stresses of life could easily prevent him.

The next day, just after noon when the cool mist of the morning had burned off and the sun streamed through the cinderblock windows to bake the clinic, he arrived. The nurse who guided him in beamed. His bandage was untouched, and his eye, swollen shut just a day ago, shone clear and bright. He was better.

Awash in gratitude, I changed his dressing, and gently probed the wound for undrained infection. I taught him how to change the bandage himself, and gave him a bag of gauze and tape for him to continue to care for the wound at home. We talked about the signs of a recurrent abscess, although my routine instructions seemed futile in this remote place, where most sick people died walking on the road to the hospital. As he took the dressing supplies, for the first time a hint of a smile alighted on his face.

Thank you for the grace of this moment, Lord, I prayed. *Please, continue to heal him.* I watched him leave until his silhouette darkened against the sunlit doorway and then disappeared. I assumed it was the last time I would see him.

Two days later, after we'd packed up our clinic and readied ourselves to return home, we joined the local pastor for Sunday worship service. We sat in plastic chairs in a single-room church of dried mud, our heads shielded from the elements by one of the corrugated tin roofs so ubiquitous throughout the continent. After we prayed and sang familiar hymns that sounded newly profound in a different tongue, I glanced about the church, thanking God for his power to bring brothers and sisters together across oceans.

Then I saw him.

He lingered at the rear of the church, his back against the door-frame, one bare foot planted on the cool wall. A new, clean dressing had carefully replaced my handiwork. After the pastor issued a benediction, we filed out of the church, and the little boy stood askance and watched. He especially studied the pastor, and an air of curiosity replaced his stoicism of previous days. The pastor felt eyes upon him, turned, and placed a hand on the boy's head. I didn't hear the words, but saw tenderness exchange between them, and I fought tears when a broad smile, the first true smile he'd shown, brightened the boy's face.

Something was stirring. The Holy Spirit had worked through a frightening ordeal, all pus and blood and blades wielded by strangers, to draw this child to God.

Glimmers of Grace

The truest and loveliest moments in medicine work like this. For all the pain and suffering we encounter in the hospital, God's love breaks through, sometimes through dramatic saves from death but more often in the simple laying on of hands. Medicine is a common means of God's kindness, and we see glimmers of his love in every tender moment. Consider the gloved handhold between a nurse and a patient on an operating table, or the song, barely audible, whispered by a mother to her newborn child. A nursing assistant offers to shave the stubble dotting a man's face after a week-long ICU stay. A doctor and a family member embrace out of joy at the birth of a child, or out of relief that a loved one has survived a cancer operation. A clinician, compelled by love, forgoes sleep at home to stand vigil all night by the bedside of a critically ill patient.

God moves through such moments to restore the broken, and to illuminate his image through us. He reminds us that our greatest callings in life are to love him and to love our neighbors as ourselves (Matt. 22:36–40). "Love one another," Jesus told his disciples, "just as I have loved you, you also are to love one another" (John 13:34). The Greek word for "love" Jesus uses in this verse is *agape*, the perfect, selfless, covenantal love that he himself shares with the Father. When we lay on hands in medicine, tend wounds, and commit ourselves to the welfare of another, we live out this commandment. We reflect to others a gleam of God's radiant love.

Yet medicine also leaves its scars. It may usher us toward recovery from a catastrophe, but like Jacob whose wrestle with God earned him a perpetual limp (Gen. 32:31), we leave the ordeal changed, the old hurts lingering. Sometimes, the scars twist and contort our flesh, declaring our trials to all. In other cases, they lurk deep within us, hidden from the world, like a silent cancer gnawing from within.

What I hope the preceding pages have demonstrated is that God's love, so evident in the successes, also persists through these hard moments, even if we can't discern how. The gospel doesn't guarantee us an easy life, free from pain. Jesus warns precisely the opposite, cautioning that we cannot follow him unless we deny ourselves and take up our cross (Matt. 16:24–25). "If they persecuted me, they will also persecute you" (John 15:20), he counsels his disciples.

Jesus told numerous parables to illustrate his teachings, but in none of them did he compare Christian discipleship to a stroll along a garden path. He doesn't promise us ease.

He does, however, offer us hope to endure. Through the cross, he grants us assurance of God's love, a promise that outlasts our most miserable sufferings.

Dear friend in Christ, when the pain sears through your limbs or clutches your heart, cling to that promise. Harbor God's word in your heart, so that when the blades of illness and death assail you, you can call upon the truth to cover you as an impenetrable shield (Eph. 6:16–17). We cannot explain away the tragedies that befall us or assuage them with our own meager words, but God's word, eternal, issuing forth in love, cures all ills. He gives us medicine as a means of grace, an extension of his love for mankind. But true healing, and true rest, that light yoke, comes only from him.

When you gaze into the mirror and find your face wan from illness and haggard from grief, remember that even as our sense of ourselves fades, *who he is* never changes. He is our provider. Our Father. He is merciful. Whatever disasters ransack the earth, he is sovereign, and his name remains blessed.

And when you look back upon the wreckage of your life, the neat margins torn by tragedy, remember *what God has done.* He has claimed you for his own. In Christ he has lavished you with love. He has secured a place for you within his glory, far from the dreary corridors of the hospital, in the new heavens and new earth where everything will be made new (Rev. 21:5). In Christ, death has no sting (1 Cor. 15:55). Through him, our bodies, now languishing, will be made whole. One day, the harsh lamps of the hospital corridor will go out, and the radiance of God's glory, resplendent in love, will light up all creation.

Cling to God's word. Harbor it in your heart, for "the word of God is living and active, sharper than any two-edged sword" (Heb. 4:12). Run to well-loved passages when fear grips you. Sing beloved hymns. When your eyes fail or your tongue sticks to the roof of your mouth, ask others to read Scripture to you. Dwell in it during the long hours of waiting. When the pain seizes you, cleave to God's word as a beacon through the darkness, carrying you home, a lamp to your feet and a light to your path (Ps. 119:105).

Cling to God's word, so you may remember. Remember his work in your life until now. But also remember who he is and what he has done in Christ.

He is the Lord your God, the Holy One of Israel, your Savior.

He has redeemed you, and has called you by name. You are his.

When you pass through the waters, however high the tide rises, he will be with you. In Christ, he will not let you fall. In Christ, you are his own forever.

Fear not, for I have redeemed you;
    I have called you by name, you are mine.
When you pass through the waters, I will be with you;
    and through the rivers, they shall not overwhelm you;
when you walk through fire you shall not be burned,
    and the flame shall not consume you.
For I am the LORD your God,
    the Holy One of Israel, your Savior. (Isa. 43:1–3)

Acknowledgments

THIS BOOK BEGAN with a prayer that I might wisely steward the testimonies God had entrusted to me. The progression from a hazy idea to the present book occurred only through the generosity of others, and by the grace of God.

I am deeply grateful to Dave DeWit from Crossway, who advocated for this work and provided so much kind encouragement. His guidance was invaluable for fine-tuning the message of this book. Dave, thank you for your wisdom and compassion, and for your long years of service stewarding words for God's glory.

To Erik Wolgemuth and colleagues at Wolgemuth and Associates, thank you for your partnership and support, for your keen insights as this project developed, and for your readiness to provide feedback along the way.

Pastor Jefrey Jensen has been instrumental to my understanding of Scripture. Pastor, thank you for sharing your gifts with our community of believers, and for always pointing us to the gospel.

To the congregation at Our Savior Lutheran Church in Topsfield, Massachusetts, especially my small group, thank you for your openness and willingness to walk together as brothers and sisters in Christ, seeking to love one another because he loved us first.

I must extend special thanks to Roxi Green-Iyawe and her dear family, for permitting me to share David's story, and for her generosity in reviewing relevant chapters even when revisiting such moments was painful. Roxi, I thank the Lord that love for our departed brother has brought us together as sisters. Blessings and love to you always!

Although I've entered a season of life away from the hospital, the memories of patients continue to shape me. I am forever grateful to those who trusted me with their care over the years. Thank you for the privilege of partnering with you through some of life's most difficult moments.

The editorial staff at the Gospel Coalition and Desiring God have extended so much encouragement, support, and wise writing counsel over the years. Thank you for your patience and guidance, and for your dedication to glorifying the Lord through the written word.

To my husband, Scottie, with whom I've now shared over half of my life, thank you for your patience and love, which anchored me through trials in the hospital and continues to hold me fast as I explore memories of them.

Finally, but most importantly, thanks be to God, who in Christ makes all things new. May his name be praised forever.

Appendix 1

Verses to Memorize for the Hospital

THOSE OF US STRUGGLING in the hospital need assurance of God's goodness and steadfast love more than ever, but a hospital stay or any ordeal with debilitating illness doesn't permit elaborate exegesis. We need the power of God's word to uplift our souls, in doses our disease-crippled minds can retain.[1]

Here are ten passages exemplifying God's love for us through Christ, to buoy you through the tempest of severe illness. Guard them in your heart.

"The LORD is my rock and my fortress and my deliverer,
    my God, my rock, in whom I take refuge,
    my shield, and the horn of my salvation, my stronghold."
    (Ps. 18:2)

"Even though I walk through the valley of the shadow of
    death,
    I will fear no evil,
for you are with me;

---

1 This appendix is adapted with permission from "Verses to Memorize for the Hospital," September 26, 2018, desiringGod.org, https://www.desiringgod.org/articles/verses-to-memorize-for-the-hospital.

your rod and your staff,
 they comfort me." (Ps. 23:4)

"God is our refuge and strength,
 a very present help in trouble.
Therefore we will not fear though the earth gives way,
 though the mountains be moved into the heart of the sea,
though its waters roar and foam,
 though the mountains tremble at its swelling." (Ps. 46:1–3)

"My flesh and my heart may fail,
 but God is the strength of my heart and my portion
 forever." (Ps. 73:26)

"I lift up my eyes to the hills.
 From where does my help come?
My help comes from the LORD,
 who made heaven and earth." (Ps. 121:1–2)

"I am the resurrection and the life. Whoever believes in me, though he die, yet shall he live, and everyone who lives and believes in me shall never die." (John 11:25–26)

"For I am sure that neither death nor life, nor angels nor rulers, nor things present nor things to come, nor powers, nor height nor depth, nor anything else in all creation, will be able to separate us from the love of God in Christ Jesus our Lord." (Rom. 8:38–39)

"Though our outer self is wasting away, our inner self is being renewed day by day. For this light momentary affliction is preparing for us an eternal weight of glory beyond all comparison, as we look not to the things that are seen but to the things that are unseen.

For the things that are seen are transient, but the things that are unseen are eternal." (2 Cor. 4:16–18)

"According to his great mercy, he has caused us to be born again to a living hope through the resurrection of Jesus Christ from the dead, to an inheritance that is imperishable, undefiled, and unfading, kept in heaven for you, who by God's power are being guarded through faith for a salvation ready to be revealed in the last time." (1 Pet. 1:3–5)

"He will wipe away every tear from their eyes, and death shall be no more, neither shall there be mourning, nor crying, nor pain anymore, for the former things have passed away. And he who was seated on the throne said, 'Behold, I am making all things new.'" (Rev. 21:4–5)

Appendix 2

Finding the Right Words

*But what comes out of the mouth proceeds from
the heart, and this defiles a person.*

MATTHEW 15:18

MINISTERING TO THE ILL allows us to love our neighbors in their vulnerable moments, and in so doing, to reflect God's mercy (Matt. 22:39; Mark 12:31; James 5:13–15). Unfortunately, too often awkwardness subverts our efforts to help the sick. In our unease, and in desperation to *fix* the situation, we fill the silence with advice or platitudes that discourage those whom we seek to uplift.[1]

As both a physician and a friend, I've failed miserably in this arena, often saying the wrong thing and witnessing the unhappy effect. Over time, those who have borne with me have outlined some points to remember.

When we pull aside the bedside curtain, the following suggestions may help to build up those we seek to love, rather than tear them down.

---

[1] This appendix is adapted with permission from "What Not to Say to Someone in the Hospital," August 25, 2018, desiringGod.org, https://www.desiringgod.org/articles/what-not-to-say-to-someone-in-the-hospital.

Six Things *Not* to Say

1. "Do you know what you should do? You should try _____."
A visit to a friend in the hospital is not the right time to recommend therapies you've learned about on Pinterest or from your cousin thrice removed. Hospitalization implies complicated illness, and it involves a constant barrage of monitoring, invasive tests, and a throng of healthcare professionals. Most people feel overwhelmed, exhausted, and scared in this environment, and to suggest a home-grown or over-the-counter remedy as the answer can be demeaning.

2. "Don't worry. You're going to be just fine."
Unless you have in-depth clinical knowledge about your friend's situation, don't promise that everything will be fine. The truth is that despite our fervent prayers, things may *not* be fine, and insisting otherwise denies people permission to voice their fears. When a friend is dealing with a very real threat to life, empty promises of recovery can downplay her concerns, abandoning her to manage her troubling thoughts alone.

Likewise, avoid militaristic euphemisms like "fight the good fight." Overcoming illness often depends on influences beyond our control, rather than on sheer tenacity. Physiology and rogue cells, not personality traits, determine disease trajectory, and when we misrepresent recovery as a matter of will, we equate worsening disease with personal failure.

3. "I know how you feel."
Even if you've suffered from a similar medical condition, don't presume to know exactly how your friend feels. Illness narratives are not universal. The experience with a given disease differs between individuals, with temperament, values, fears, and past experiences

all exerting influence. Instead of assuring a friend of your under-standing, *ask* how he or she feels. *Listen* and *sympathize*. The focus should be on your friend, not on you.

4. "Let me know if I can help in any way."
This seems like a benign and perhaps even helpful question at first glance. But danger lurks in the phrasing. First of all, it rings insincere. Second, it demands that an ailing and already overwhelmed friend determine how you can be useful.

Those hospitalized *do* need help. They need fellowship and reminders that their disease does not define them. They need people to manage the mundane responsibilities of life that tumble onward while they lie stranded at the hospital—the accumulating bills, the empty pet dishes, the garden wilting in the backyard. *But the burden for delegating help shouldn't fall upon the one suffering in the hospital.* Don't ask a friend to contact you if needed; instead, think of what she might need, and volunteer. Better yet, be the kind of friend for whom barriers to asking don't exist.

5. "You look great/terrible!"
Comments on appearance reflect our own preconceived notions rather than a sick friend's progress. In the best-case scenario they offer little solace, and in the worst, they denigrate. Whatever the angle, talking about physical appearance may dissuade a friend from telling you how he's actually doing. Looking great and feeling great are separate issues.

6. Anything to the medical team without your friend's permission. Unless she explicitly asks you to stay, excuse yourself from the room when your friend's doctor arrives. The daily fodder of medical practice involves sensitive and private questions, and she may feel

uncomfortable answering in your presence. Visiting doesn't grant you privileges of information. Respect her privacy.

Five Ways to Help

Those struggling with illness desperately need reminders of God's grace. Listening and hearing, rather than opining and speaking, are more effective tools for witnessing for the gospel in the hospital setting.

The following points can help guide us:

1. Pray.
Cover your sick friend with prayer. Pray with him. Pray for him. Assure him that you regularly lift him up to our risen Lord, who makes all things new (Rev. 21:5).

2. Practice the ministry of presence.
On some days, a friend may need to work out her worries with you. On others, she may simply appreciate a companion to sit beside her as she watches TV. In all cases, aim to follow her lead and to support rather than to fix. Be available, listen to what she says, and offer sympathy. Be with her because you love her for the unique, wonderfully made image bearer God fashioned her to be. Treat her as a sister in Christ rather than as a project.

3. Be mindful of the patient's needs above yours.
Struggling with illness is exhausting. Don't visit unless your friend has confirmed he wants company. Pay attention to nonverbal cues, and make an exit when he appears weary. Ask him what's helpful and what isn't. Invite him to tell you when to leave. Above all, *listen* to his needs. Sympathize, then listen some more. Let him direct the tenor of the visit.

4. Infuse God's word into visits.

When selected carefully, Scripture can buoy those sinking into despair. Psalms and hymns wield restorative power. This is not the time for lengthy exegesis and Bible study, but short passages that highlight God's grace and our hope in Christ can uplift a friend in a hospital gown. Offering to read Scripture is especially important for those whose illness disallows them to read the Bible on their own. Bring audio books of the Bible for when you leave. Offer to sing well-loved hymns together. Help them harbor the word in their heart.

5. Reaffirm your friend's identity in Christ.

Don't let illness subsume your friend's identity. Treat her as you always did before she fell ill. Joke with her as you always would. Discuss mutual friends, favorite memories, the ordinary stuff of life. Never speak to her as though illness has changed *who she is*, but rather reaffirm that through faith in Christ she is renewed. Remind her that she is blameless before and treasured by the Great Physician, who heals the world through his wounds.

Glossary

adrenaline—Also known as epinephrine, a hormone that increases blood pressure and quickens heartbeat

artery—A blood vessel that carries blood away from the heart to supply tissues and organs with oxygen

bronchial tree—The passageways that transport air from the trachea to the lungs

bronchoscopy—A procedure, both diagnostic and therapeutic, whereby a camera is threaded into the airways

capillaries—Fine branching blood vessels that form a network between vessels carrying blood to and from the heart

cardiac arrest—When the heart fails to circulate blood flow effectively, either from abnormal rhythm, inadequate blood volume, poor pump function of the heart, or obstruction to blood flow

cardiopulmonary resuscitation (CPR)—Emergency chest compressions and ventilation to maintain blood flow to the brain when cardiac arrest occurs

cardiovascular—Pertaining to the heart and blood vessels

catheter—A flexible tube inserted into a body cavity or blood vessel

cerebral—Concerning the brain

chronic obstructive pulmonary disease (COPD)—A group of lung diseases that block air flow and make it difficult to breathe; emphysema is a form of COPD

clotting factors—Enzymes that work together to form a blood clot after an injury

computed tomography (CT) scan—A diagnostic imaging test that creates detailed cross-sectional images of tissue and internal organs

delirium—Acute confusion that waxes and wanes, often accompanied by delusions, paranoia, and hallucinations

electrolytes—Minerals with an electric charge (e.g., calcium, magnesium, potassium, sodium) that play a vital role in functions throughout the body

emphysema—A variant of chronic obstructive pulmonary disease (COPD) in which the air sacs of the lungs are damaged and enlarged

endotracheal tube—A silicone tube placed into the windpipe for mechanical ventilation

enzyme—A protein that acts as a catalyst in a biochemical reaction

extracorporeal membrane oxygenation (ECMO)—A machine that replaces the function of the heart and lungs

fibrin—A protein critical to blood clotting and wound healing

hemorrhage—Bleeding

hospice—A philosophy of care that focuses on palliation of symptoms at the end of life, with emphasis on quality of life and spiritual and physical well-being

hysterectomy—Surgical removal of the uterus

intensive care unit (ICU)—The department in a hospital where the most seriously ill patients are constantly observed

intravenous (IV)—Administered through the bloodstream, via access in a vein

lidocaine—A local anesthetic agent, used to numb the skin during minor surgical procedures

mechanical ventilator—A machine that provides breathing support

neuron—A nerve cell, located in the brain, spinal cord, or peripheral nervous system

orthopedic—Pertaining to the bones

palliative care—An approach to medical care that focuses on improvement in quality of life, at all stages of illness

peritonitis—Inflammation of the lining of the abdomen, usually from infection

platelets—Cell fragments that circulate throughout the bloodstream and play an essential role in normal blood clotting

quadriplegia—The paralysis of all four limbs

right ventricle—The chamber of the heart that pumps blood to the lungs to receive oxygen

saline—A fluid consisting of water and salt, used to replace lost volume in dehydration

sepsis—A widespread response to infection that reduces blood flow to organs and threatens life

shock—A condition characterized by inadequate blood flow to organs, resulting in poor oxygen delivery and death if untreated

suture—Surgical material used to close a wound or repair tissue, or the process of placing stitches

trachea—Medical term for windpipe

tracheostomy—Surgical placement of a tube through the neck and into the windpipe, to permit connection to a mechanical ventilator

transfusion—The infusion of donated blood products

ultrasound—A diagnostic imaging technique that uses sound waves

ventilation—Air exchange in breathing, specifically removal of carbon dioxide from the bloodstream

Further Reading

Balboni, Michael J. and Tracy A. *Hostility to Hospitality: Spirituality and Professional Socialization within Medicine*. New York, NY: Oxford University Press, 2019.
This book is highly academic, but is an excellent resource for those interested in studies on spirituality and medicine in America.

Card, Michael. *A Sacred Sorrow: Reaching Out to God in the Lost Language of Lament*. Colorado Springs, CO: NavPress, 2005.
A beautifully written and theologically rich exploration of biblical expressions of lament, with extrapolations to modern struggles with grief.

Cole, Cameron. *Therefore I Have Hope: 12 Truths That Comfort, Sustain, and Redeem in Tragedy*. Wheaton, IL: Crossway, 2018.
In 2013, Cameron Cole and his wife lost their three-year-old son to sudden death. In this heartfelt book, Cole combines his sensitivity as a father with his careful eye for theology to offer practical, biblical help for the grieving.

Dunlop, John, MD. *Finishing Well to the Glory of God: Strategies from a Christian Physician*. Wheaton, IL: Crossway, 2011.

Dr. Dunlop offers believers a beautiful, tenderly written guide to resting in the arms of Christ at the end of life. He weaves medical advice throughout a narrative that at some points reads like a memoir and at other times like a devotional.

Elliot, Elisabeth. *Suffering Is Never for Nothing.* Nashville, TN: B&H, 2019.

Published posthumously and drawn from a collection of her lectures, this poignant exploration of suffering is a beautiful blend of theology and personal experience from one of Christendom's most gifted authors.

Guthrie, Nancy. *Hearing Jesus Speak into Your Sorrow.* Carol Stream, IL: Tyndale House, 2009.

Having lost two infant children to a genetic condition, Guthrie is well-acquainted with grief. In this beautiful work, she guides us in looking to Jesus when sorrow grips us.

Power, Philip Bennet. *A Book of Comfort for Those in Sickness.* Edinburgh, Scotland: Banner of Truth, 2018.

This little book is over a hundred years old, but its counsel is just as relevant today. Power, a minister with the Church of England in the 1800s, offers wise guidance in leaning upon God when illness strips us of hope and independence.

Risner, Vaneetha Rendall. *The Scars That Have Shaped Me: How God Meets Us in Suffering.* Minneapolis, MN: Desiring God, 2016.

Vaneetha Rendall Risner has weathered more seasons of suffering than most experience in a lifetime. In this collection of reflections, she points to Christ as our hope and our solace as we endure heartache and pain.

Vroegop, Mark. *Dark Clouds, Deep Mercy: Discovering the Grace of Lament*. Wheaton, IL: Crossway, 2019.

Having endured tragedy himself, pastor Mark Vroegop takes a deep dive into lamentation in the Bible, offering readers clarity and practical guidance as they bring their grievances to God.

General Index

John, 27
Jonah, 34, 54, 93
Joseph, 65
Joshua, 14
joy, 100, 121, 189
justice, 130, 154, 170

Kenya, 185
Koran, 145

law, 154
Lazarus, 84–85
lidocaine, 186, 206
life, and water, 168–69, 172–73
life expectancy, 40
light, 164, 165
listening, 201, 202
liturgy, 34
loneliness, 25
Lord's Supper, 36, 156
love, 12–13, 46, 62, 178

manna, 13, 54, 66
Martha, 84–85, 88
Mary (sister of Martha), 84–85, 88
meaning, 25, 76–78
mechanical ventilator, 20, 43, 206, 207
medicine
  and grace, 15, 188–89
  and technology, 39–40
  wilderness of, 22–26
mercy, 22, 37, 53, 77, 93–97, 199
militaristic euphemisms, 200
Miller, Sherry, 26
ministry of presence, 202
miracles, 40–42, 85, 142
mortality, 23, 26, 34
Moses, 14, 16, 35, 66–67, 110, 152, 154, 170–71
mourning, 75, 85, 148, 197

Nebuchadnezzar, 131
neighbors, 36–37, 83, 189, 199
neonatal ICU (NICU), 57–69
neurologists, 144
neuron, 100, 144, 207
new covenant, 132–33
new heavens and new earth, 78
Ninevites, 93–96
Noah, 54, 110
nominal Christian, 11, 120
nourishment, 63–65

obedience, 93
ordinary means of grace, 44
orthopedic, 207
"outlier," 144
oxygen, 101, 102, 152–53, 168

pain, 20, 34, 137, 148, 162, 175, 190
palliative care, 177, 206, 207
pancreatitis, 169
paper cuts, 127–28
parable of the prodigal son, 61–62
paralysis, 160
paranoia, 111, 177, 178
Passover, 155–56
Paul, 49–50, 61, 83–84, 92, 103, 131–32, 139, 165, 171
peritonitis, 90, 207
Perry, Jackie Hill, 15
Peter, 27
physical appearance, 201
physiology, 21, 200
Pinterest, 200
platelets, 41, 42, 153, 207
platitudes, 199
pneumonia, 69–70, 102, 109
power, of God, 44–46
prayer, 21, 22, 23, 33, 34, 82–88, 142, 144, 202

Scripture Index

Also Available
from Kathryn Butler

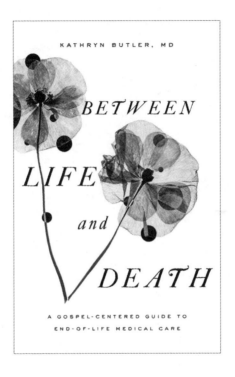

KATHRYN BUTLER, MD

BETWEEN

LIFE

and

DEATH

A GOSPEL-CENTERED GUIDE TO
END-OF-LIFE MEDICAL CARE

"Dr. Butler has woven together a clear explanation of detailed
and complex medical issues with an intimate knowledge
of Scripture to bring forth a book of immense value for
patients, loved ones, and clergy as they face the seemingly
insurmountable questions of ICU and end-of-life care. It is
well written, illustrated with real-life dilemmas, and oozing
with compassion, both her own and that of our Savior."

ROBERT D. ORR, MD, CM, clinical ethicist;
author, *Medical Ethics and the Faith Factor*

For more information, visit **crossway.org**.